First World War
and Army of Occupation
War Diary
France, Belgium and Germany

4 DIVISION
11 Infantry Brigade
Royal Irish Regiment
2nd Battalion
1 March 1915 - 31 May 1916

WO95/1497/2

The Naval & Military Press Ltd
www.nmarchive.com
Published in association with The National Archives

Published by

The Naval & Military Press Ltd

Unit 10 Ridgewood Industrial Park,

Uckfield, East Sussex,

TN22 5QE England

Tel: +44 (0) 1825 749494

www.naval-military-press.com

www.nmarchive.com

This diary has been reprinted in facsimile from the original. Any imperfections are inevitably reproduced and the quality may fall short of modern type and cartographic standards.

© **Crown Copyright**
Images reproduced by permission of The National Archives, London, England, 2015.

Contents

Document type	Place/Title	Date From	Date To
Heading	WO95/1497 4th Div 11 Inf Bde 2 Bn Royal Irish Regt March 1915-May 1916		
Heading	11th Infantry Bde 2nd Royal First Reg. January To May, 1916		
Heading	2nd R First Reg. Mar To July		
Heading	4th Div 12th Inf. Bde. 2nd Battn. The Royal Irish Regt. March 1915		
War Diary	St. Omer	01/03/1915	09/03/1915
War Diary	Wisques	09/03/1915	12/03/1915
War Diary	Hazebrook	13/03/1915	13/03/1915
War Diary	Bailleul	14/03/1915	14/03/1915
War Diary	Ploegstreet	14/03/1915	14/03/1915
War Diary	Le Bizet	15/03/1915	31/03/1915
Miscellaneous	Appendix I		
Miscellaneous	Appendix No.		
Operation(al) Order(s)	Operation Order No 2. By Brigadier General F.G. Anley. Commanding 12th Infantry Brigade.	22/03/1915	22/03/1915
Diagram etc	German Line		
Heading	4th Div. 12th Inf. Bde. 2nd Battn. The Royal Irish Regt. April 1915		
War Diary	Le Bizet	01/04/1915	01/04/1915
War Diary	Ploegsteert	02/04/1915	03/04/1915
War Diary	Ploegsteert	04/04/1915	30/04/1915
Miscellaneous	12th Brigade Operation Order	08/04/1915	08/04/1915
Miscellaneous	Programme.		
Miscellaneous	2nd. Bn. The Royal Irish Regiment.		
Miscellaneous			
Miscellaneous	Readjustment Of 12th Brigade Line.		
Heading	4th Div. 12th Inf. Bde. 2nd Battn. The Royal Irish Regt. May 1915		
Miscellaneous	2 R Irish Regiment To Go To IV Division 11th Brigade		
War Diary	Trenches	01/05/1915	09/05/1915
War Diary	Rest Billets	10/05/1915	13/05/1915
War Diary	Trenches	14/05/1915	16/05/1915
War Diary	Chateau	17/05/1915	17/05/1915
War Diary	Rest Billets	18/05/1915	20/05/1915
War Diary	Vlamertinge	21/05/1915	21/05/1915
War Diary	Yser Canal	22/05/1915	22/05/1915
War Diary	Trenches	23/05/1915	23/05/1915
War Diary	First Farm	24/05/1915	24/05/1915
War Diary	Trenches	24/05/1915	24/05/1915
War Diary	First Farm	24/05/1915	24/05/1915
War Diary	La Brique	25/05/1915	25/05/1915
War Diary	La Brique Yser Canal	25/05/1915	31/05/1915
Miscellaneous	2nd Bn. The Royal Irish Regiment.		
Map			
Heading	4th Div. 12th Inf. Bde. 2nd Battn. The Royal Irish Regt. June 1915		
War Diary	Yeast Canal Rose Billets	01/06/1915	18/06/1915
War Diary	Yser Canal	19/06/1915	30/06/1915

Heading	2nd Battn. The Royal Irish Regt. July 1915		
War Diary	Yser Canal	01/07/1915	04/07/1915
War Diary	Chateau Trois Tours	05/07/1915	08/07/1915
War Diary	Proven	09/07/1915	13/07/1915
War Diary	St Jans Capell	13/07/1915	21/07/1915
War Diary	Godversvelde	22/07/1915	22/07/1915
War Diary	Train	22/07/1915	22/07/1915
War Diary	Freschvillers	23/07/1915	23/07/1915
War Diary	Louvencourt	24/07/1915	30/07/1915
War Diary	Acheux	30/07/1915	31/07/1915
Miscellaneous	A Form. Messages And Signals		
Miscellaneous	12th Brigade No. B.M. 76		
Miscellaneous	A Form. Messages And Signals		
Operation(al) Order(s)	12th Brigade Operation Order No. 2	06/07/1915	06/07/1915
Miscellaneous	Reliefs On Night 7/8 July, 1915		
Miscellaneous	4th Div. Q/115		
Miscellaneous	A Form. Messages And Signals		
Miscellaneous	4th Div. Q/639	19/07/1915	19/07/1915
Miscellaneous	Table Showing Allocation Of Units To Trains And Hours Of Departure.		
Miscellaneous	Detrainment 4th Division Appendix XI		
Miscellaneous	Appendix XII		
Heading	4th Division 2nd Royal Irish Regt Joined From The 12th Bde 26-7-15 Less September August To December 1915		
Heading	2nd Battn. The Royal Irish Regt. August 1915		
War Diary	Acheux	01/08/1915	07/08/1915
War Diary	Englebelmer	08/08/1915	19/08/1915
War Diary	Mesnil	20/08/1915	25/08/1915
War Diary	Englebelmer Trenches	26/08/1915	30/08/1915
Miscellaneous	C Form (Original). Messages And Signals.		
Map			
Heading	2nd Battn. The Royal Irish Regt. September 1915		
Heading	2nd Battn. The Royal Irish Regt. October 1915		
War Diary	Englebelmer	01/10/1915	31/10/1915
Heading	2nd Battn. The Royal Irish Regt. November 1915		
War Diary	Englebelmer	01/11/1915	30/11/1915
Miscellaneous	A Form. Messages And Signals		
Miscellaneous	C Form (Quadruplicate). Messages And Signals.		
Miscellaneous	C Form (Original). Messages And Signals.		
Miscellaneous	C Form (Duplicate). Messages And Signals.		
Miscellaneous	C Form (Original). Messages And Signals.		
Heading	2nd Battn. The Royal Irish Regt. December 1915		
War Diary	Englebelmer	01/12/1915	31/12/1915
Miscellaneous	C Form (Original). Messages And Signals.		
Heading	2nd Battalion Royal Irish Regiment January 1916		
War Diary	Englebelmer	01/01/1916	30/01/1916
Heading	2nd Battalion Royal Irish Regiment February 1916		
War Diary	Englebelmer	01/02/1916	29/02/1916
Miscellaneous	C Form (Original). Messages And Signals.		
Operation(al) Order(s)	Operation Order No. 1. By Lieut. Colonel W. J. Dugan, D.S.O., Commanding 2nd. Bn. The Royal Irish Regiment.	06/02/1916	06/02/1916
Operation(al) Order(s)	Operation Order No. 2. By Lieut. Colonel W. J. Dugan, D.S.O., Commanding 2nd. Bn. The Royal Irish Regiment.	07/02/1916	07/02/1916

Operation(al) Order(s)	Operation Order No. 3. By Lieut. Colonel W. J. Dugan, D.S.O., Commanding 2nd. Bn. The Royal Irish Regiment.	09/02/1916	09/02/1916
Operation(al) Order(s)	Operation Order No. 4. By Lieut. Colonel W. J. Dugan, D.S.O., Commanding 2nd. Bn. The Royal Irish Regiment.	17/02/1916	17/02/1916
Operation(al) Order(s)	2nd Bn the Royal Irish Regt. Order No 5. Reference France Sheet 51c.		
Heading	2nd Battalion Royal Irish Regiment March 1916		
War Diary	Grouches	01/03/1916	31/03/1916
Operation(al) Order(s)	2nd Battalion The Royal Irish Regiment. Order No. 6	05/03/1916	05/03/1916
Miscellaneous	Telegramme		
Miscellaneous	Signification des principales Indications eventuelles pouvant Figurer en Tete De l'adresse		
Miscellaneous	Telegramme		
Miscellaneous	Indications de Service		
Miscellaneous	C Form (Duplicate). Messages And Signals.		
Operation(al) Order(s)	2nd Battalion The Royal Irish Regiment Order No 6	18/03/1916	18/03/1916
Operation(al) Order(s)	2nd Battalion The Royal Irish Regiment Operation Order No. 7	19/03/1916	19/03/1916
Miscellaneous			
Operation(al) Order(s)	2nd Bn The Royal Irish Regiment Order No. 8	23/03/1916	23/03/1916
Miscellaneous	Issued With Order No. 8	23/03/1916	23/03/1916
Operation(al) Order(s)	2nd Battalion The Royal Irish Regt. Order No. 9	26/03/1916	26/03/1916
Miscellaneous	A Form. Messages And Signals		
Operation(al) Order(s)	2nd Battalion The Royal Irish Regiment Order No. 10	29/03/1916	29/03/1916
Heading	2nd Royal Irish Regiment April 1916		
War Diary		01/04/1916	30/04/1916
Miscellaneous	C Form (Duplicate). Messages And Signals.		
Miscellaneous	A Form. Messages And Signals		
Miscellaneous			
Miscellaneous	A Form. Messages And Signals		
Miscellaneous	C Form (Original). Messages And Signals.		
Miscellaneous	C Form (Duplicate). Messages And Signals.		
Miscellaneous	C Form (Original). Messages And Signals.		
Miscellaneous	C Form (Duplicate). Messages And Signals.		
Miscellaneous	C Form (Original). Messages And Signals.		
Miscellaneous	C Form (Duplicate). Messages And Signals.		
Operation(al) Order(s)	2nd Battalion The Royal Irish Regiment. Order No. 11	04/04/1916	04/04/1916
Miscellaneous	2nd Bn. The Royal Irish Regiment Order No. 12-10th April 1916	10/04/1916	10/04/1916
Operation(al) Order(s)	2nd Battalion, The Royal Irish Regiment Order No. 13-16/4/16	16/04/1916	16/04/1916
Miscellaneous	Secret		
Miscellaneous	2nd Bn. The Royal Irish Regiment.		
Miscellaneous			
Operation(al) Order(s)	2nd Bn. The Royal Irish Regiment. Order No. 14-22/04/16	22/04/1916	22/04/1916
Operation(al) Order(s)	2nd. Bn The Royal Irish Regt. Order No 15	28/04/1916	28/04/1916
Heading	2nd Battalion Royal Irish Regiment May 1916		
War Diary	Fonquevillers	01/05/1916	01/05/1916
War Diary	Souastre	02/05/1916	03/05/1916
War Diary	Halloy	04/05/1916	06/05/1916
War Diary	Bernaville	06/05/1916	15/05/1916
War Diary	Cramont	16/05/1916	21/05/1916
War Diary	Bernaville	21/05/1916	21/05/1916

War Diary	La Vicogne	22/05/1916	22/05/1916
War Diary	Morlancourt	22/05/1916	25/05/1916
War Diary	Bois D'Estailles	25/05/1916	25/05/1916
War Diary	C 2 Sub Sector	27/05/1916	31/05/1916
Miscellaneous	2nd. Battalion The Royal Irish Regiment. Daily Summary. 28/5/16	28/05/1916	28/05/1916
Miscellaneous	2nd. Battalion The Royal Irish Regiment. Daily Summary. 29/5/16	29/05/1916	29/05/1916
Miscellaneous	2nd. Battalion The Royal Irish Regiment. Daily Summary. 30/05/16	30/05/1916	30/05/1916
Miscellaneous	2nd. Battalion The Royal Irish Regiment. Daily Summary. 31/5/16	31/05/1916	31/05/1916
Miscellaneous			
Operation(al) Order(s)	2nd Bde. The Royal Irish Regiment Order No. 16	01/05/1916	01/05/1916
Operation(al) Order(s)	2nd Pro. The Royal Irish Regiment Order No. 16	01/05/1916	01/05/1916
Operation(al) Order(s)	2nd Bn. The Royal Irish Regiment Order No 17	02/05/1916	02/05/1916
Operation(al) Order(s)	Battalion Order No 5. By Lieut Colonel W. J. Dugan D.S.O., Commanding 2nd Battn The Royal Irish Regiment	05/05/1916	05/05/1916
Operation(al) Order(s)	2nd Bn. The Royal Irish Regt. Order No. 18	05/05/1916	05/05/1916
Operation(al) Order(s)	11th Infantry Brigade. Operation Order No. 7	05/05/1916	05/05/1916
Miscellaneous	March Table		
Operation(al) Order(s)	2nd Battn Royal Irish Regiment Operation Order No 19	14/05/1916	14/05/1916
Operation(al) Order(s)	2nd Battn. The Royal Irish Regt. Order No. 20	19/05/1916	19/05/1916
Operation(al) Order(s)	2nd Battn. The Royal Irish Regt. Order No. 21	20/05/1916	20/05/1916
Miscellaneous	B.M. 797		
Miscellaneous	March Table		
Operation(al) Order(s)	2nd Battn. The Royal Irish Regt. Order No. 22	21/05/1916	21/05/1916
Miscellaneous	Lt. Col Dugan DSO		
Operation(al) Order(s)	2nd Battalion. The Royal Irish Regiment. Operation Order No. 23	24/05/1916	24/05/1916
Operation(al) Order(s)	2nd Battalion. The Royal Irish Regiment. Operation Order No. 24	26/05/1916	26/05/1916

WO 95 /1497

4 DIV 11 Inf Bde

2 Bn Royal Irish ~~Patriot~~ Regt

Mar 1915 - May 1916

(Sept, Oct 1915 missing)

4th Division
11th Infantry Bde
2nd Royal Irish Reg.

January, To May,
1916

To 7 DIV   22 BDE

4th Division

"War Diaries"

11th ~~10th~~ Infantry Bde

2nd R. Irish Reg. Mar to July
Joined from G.H.Q. 14-3-15
Transferred to 11 Bde 26-7-15

1915 MAR — 1915 JULY

From 3 Div 8 Bde

4th Div.
12th Inf. Bde.

WAR DIARY

2ND BATTN. THE ROYAL IRISH REGT.

MARCH

1915.

WAR DIARY or INTELLIGENCE SUMMARY

Army Form C. 2118.

(Erase heading not required.)

Instructions regarding War Diaries and Intelligence Summaries are contained in F. S. Regs., Part II. and the Staff Manual respectively. Title pages will be prepared in manuscript.

Hour, Date, Place	Summary of Events and Information	Remarks and references to Appendices
6 am 8.3.15 ST OMER	Battalion moved to WISQUES, distance about 4 miles arrived about 11 am and billeted —	Order of Movers [?] shown in Appendix I
9.3.15 WISQUES	Warning order received from Battalion "to be ready to march apparently in 3 days or so. Brigade".	Baptism at WISQUES was occupied by [?] [?] [?] march [?]
1 pm 10.3.15 "	Orders received to proceed to LE BIZET to form 12th Brigade, 4th Division, 3rd Corps, 2nd Army —	[?] by [?] but might cause any [?] to [?] and equipment [?]
9 am 11.3.15 "	Marched to HAZEBROUCK distance about 18 miles. [4 mark?] noman fell out. Weather was rather snow in the field, march throughout good. Arrived at Ordnance excellent arrived at HAZEBROUCK at 4.30 pm and billeted in town. —	[?]
6 am 12.3.15 HAZEBROUCK	The Battalion was addressed by Gen. Sir H. SMITH-DORRIEN and marched to BAILLEUL where [?] arrived about 3.30 pm distance about	

WAR DIARY
or
INTELLIGENCE SUMMARY
(Erase heading not required.)

Army Form C. 2118.

Hour, Date, Place	Summary of Events and Information	Remarks and references to Appendices
3.30 pm 13 March. BAILLEUL	10 mile Battalion Route march in town. Lieut. V. E. WARD SIMPSON returned from sick leave	↓
9.15 am 14 March. BAILLEUL	Marched to LE BIZET (about one mile N. of ARMENTIERES) and joined 12 Brigade with 2Bn ESSEX REGT 2/Bn LANCASHIRE FUSILIERS, 2Bn KINGS OWN LANCASTER REGT 1/Bn MONMOUTH REGT (TF) 5th Bn. 5th LANCASHIRE REGT (TF) arrived LE BIZET about 1 PM. 2/LIEUT R H FRANKENBURG rejoined from hospital. Halves of Bn and Bde HQ are billeted in entire down at C. Edwin & HQ Coy in nunnery at PLOEGSTREET	↓
3 PM -14- PLOEGSTREET	Slight artillery fire in nunnery St hitts nunnery by 6 HQ Coy.	↓
3.30 PM 15.3.15 LE BIZET	Capt Lieutenant Frankenburg of LE BIZET LIEUT. W. GODDEN rejoined from sick list LIEUT L.W. BATCHELOR to such ambulance	↓

WAR DIARY
or
INTELLIGENCE SUMMARY
(Erase heading not required.)

Army Form C. 2118.

Instructions regarding War Diaries and Intelligence Summaries are contained in F. S. Regs., Part II. and the Staff Manual respectively. Title pages will be prepared in manuscript.

Hour, Date, Place	Summary of Events and Information	Remarks and references to Appendices
24 March 1915 AT BREST	A & B Companies in trenches. 1 man wounded.	Yt
20/3/15	C & D Companies in trenches. Slight bombardment in morning. 2 privates and Lieut. Lieut. E M PHILLIPS to hospital. Lt. Gn. MAHONY Connaught army to transport men operation orders issued	Yt
2 PM		Appendix II
9 AM 23/3/15	A & B Companies in trenches. No men wounded.	Yt
24/3/15	C & D Companies in trenches. 1 man killed.	Yt
6 PM 24/3/15	A & B Companies to trenches N. of the River WARNAVE in accordance with operation order Appendix II. C & D Companies from reserve.	See Appendix II. Night ordered trenches taken over.
25/3/15	Lieut. R. MARTIN, 3 ROYAL MUNSTER DUBLIN FUS. and 4. D. McKAY 4/ CONNAUGHT joined for attachment. Quiet during night. No man wounded. —	Yt

Army Form C. 2118.

WAR DIARY
or
INTELLIGENCE SUMMARY
(Erase heading not required.)

Instructions regarding War Diaries and Intelligence Summaries are contained in F. S. Regs., Part II. and the Staff Manual respectively. Title pages will be prepared in manuscript.

Hour, Date, Place	Summary of Events and Information	Remarks and references to Appendices

Army Form C. 2118.

WAR DIARY or INTELLIGENCE SUMMARY

(Erase heading not required.)

DISTRIBUTION OF OFFICERS SERVING WITH 2ND BN. THE ROYAL IRISH REGIMENT ON 10TH MARCH, 1915.

HEADQUARTERS.

Major R.G.S. MORIARTY,   Commanding Battalion.
Captain J.H. CHRISTIE,   Senior Major. (4« Battn)
Lieut. T.W. FITZPATRICK,   Adjutant.
  ,,   J. GLASCOTT,   Machine Gun Officer.(4/N.Staff.R)
  ,,   W.H.S. BERRY,   Scout Officer. (4/R/Inns.Fus)
  ,,   T. MAHONY,   Quarter Master.
2/Lieut. E.M. PHILLIPS,   Transport Officer.

Captain W.M. FITZMAURICE,   R.C.Chaplain.
2/Lieut. J.H.A. NEVILL,   Interpreter.(Corps of Interpreters)

Army Form C. 2118.

Appendix I Cont.

WAR DIARY
or
INTELLIGENCE SUMMARY
(Erase heading not required.)

Summary of Events and Information	Remarks and references to Appendices

"A" COMPANY.

Captain T.C. FITZHUGH, Commanding.
2/Lieut. A.R. NEWTON KING. (4/Royal Dublin Fus.)
,, M.C. MACSWEENEY. (3rd Bn. R.I.Regt)
,, A.L. RAMSAY.

"B" COMPANY.

Captain M. WICKHAM, Commanding. (Conn. Rangers.)
2/Lieut. G.C.N. STOPFORD. (3rd Bn R.I. Regt)
,, E.R.K. WHITE.

"C" COMPANY.

Captain J.D. MORROGH, Commanding. (3rd Bn. R.I. Regt)
Lieut. P.L. BLAKE. (3rd Bn. R.I. Regt)
2/Lieut. W.P. HINTON. ,, ,,
,, M.K. ANDERSON.

"D" COMPANY.

Captain C.A. FRENCH, Commanding.
Lieut. J.S. LUCKETT.
2/Lieut. J.P. MCLOUGHLIN. (4/Royal Dublin Fus.)
,, A.S. PIM. (3rd Bn R.I. Regt)
,, Sir C.P. HUNTINGTON, Bart. (3rd Bn. R.I. Regt)

Hour, Date, Place	

Instructions regarding War Diaries and Intelligence Summaries are contained in F.S. Regs., Part II. and the Staff Manual respectively. Title pages will be prepared in manuscript.

Army Form C. 2118.

WAR DIARY
INTELLIGENCE SUMMARY
(Erase heading not required.)

Instructions regarding War Diaries and Intelligence Summaries are contained in F. S. Regs., Part II. and the Staff Manual respectively. Title pages will be prepared in manuscript.

Hour, Date, Place	Summary of Events and Information	Remarks and references to Appendices
	APPENDIX No. 1	
	HONOURS AND AWARDS.	
	DISTINGUISHED CONDUCT MEDAL.	
	No. 5637 Regtl. Qr. Mr. Sergt. (Now Lieut. & Adjutant) T.W.Fitzpatrick.	
	MENTIONED IN DESPATCHES.	
	2nd. Lieutenant H. G. O. Downing. (_____ _____ _____)	

Appendix II

Copy No. 4

OPERATION ORDER No. 2.
by
Brigadier General F.G. Anley.
Commanding 12th Infantry Brigade.

22-3-1915.

1. On 24th instant when 2nd Essex Regt. are relieved from trenches 2nd Monmouths will take over the trenches now held by 2nd Essex South of the River WARNAVE and 2nd Royal Irish Regt. will take over with two Companies those North of the River WARNAVE.

2. On 28th instant 2nd Monmouths will be relieved by 2nd Essex and the two Companies Royal Irish Regt will be relieved by the other two Companies of the same Battalion, subsequent reliefs taking place at intervals of four days.

3. For purposes of tactical command only, the two Companies Royal Irish Regt. will be under the orders of 2nd Essex or 2nd Monmouths whichever is in the trenches.

Officer Commanding Royal Irish Regt. will arrange for supplies, ammunition, material, tools etc. to be sent up to his Companies in trenches and for this purpose will not use the road leading past Essex H.Q. and DESPIERRE Farm.

4. Officer Commanding 5th South Lancs will place at disposal of Officer Commanding 2nd Monmouths 100 men including proportion of Officers and N.C.O's from evening of 24th instant until evening of 27th instant.

Officer Commanding 2nd Monmouths will inform O.C. 5th South Lancs time and place at which these men are to parade.

Captain,
Brigade Major, 12th Infantry Brigade.

Issued at 6/u p.m.

Copy No. 1 filed.
" " 2 to 2nd Essex.
" " 3 to 2nd Monmouths.
" " 4 to Royal Irish Regt.
" " 5 to South Lancs.
" " 6 to King's Own.
" " 7 to Lan: Fus:

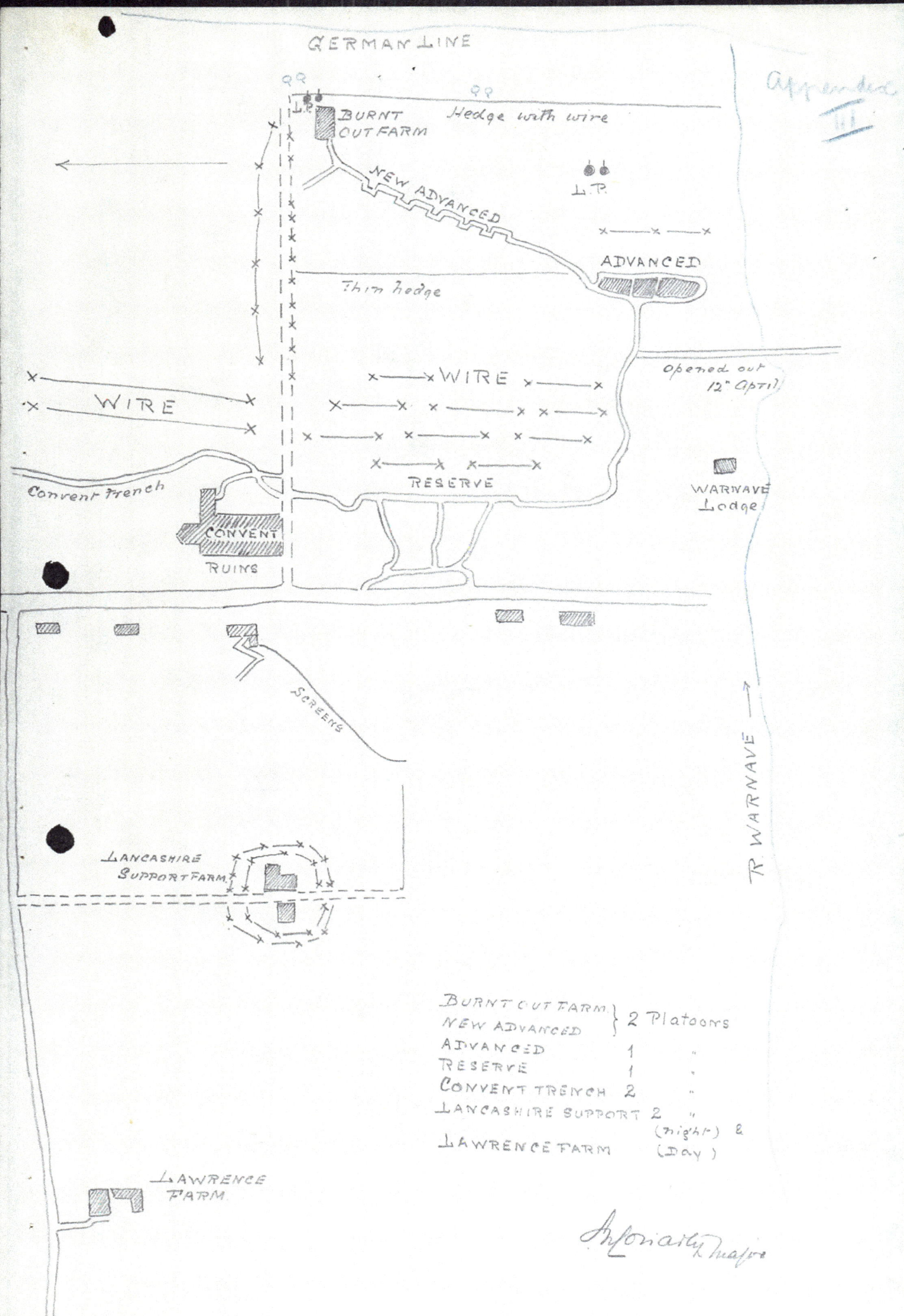

4th Div.
12th Inf.Bde.

WAR DIARY

2ND BATTN. THE ROYAL IRISH REGT.

A P R I L

1 9 1 5

WAR DIARY or INTELLIGENCE SUMMARY

Army Form C. 2118.

(Erase heading not required.)

Hour, Date, Place	Summary of Events and Information	Remarks and references to Appendices
1 April 1915 Le Bizet	Battalion moved to billets in PLOEGSTEERT —	
4pm PLOEGSTEERT	A + B Companies to trenches in relief of D + C Coys. 1 man killed.	
2 April 1915	C + D Companies in trenches. 1 man wounded	
3 April 1915	C + D in trenches. 1 man wounded 1 man	
	P.R.M.D	
4 April 1915 PLOEGSTEERT	C + D Companies in trenches. LIEUT P.L. BIRKE to ENGLAND	
	Heavy D + Hdqrs shelled. A + B proceeded to trenches in relief of "A" + "B" Companies —	
	10th Coy in trenches one man wounded. LIEUT GUINNESS went to man joined.	

Army Form C. 2118.

WAR DIARY
or
INTELLIGENCE SUMMARY
(Erase heading not required.)

Hour, Date, Place	Summary of Events and Information	Remarks and references to Appendices
4 April 1915. PLOEGSTEERT	4 "B" Company in trenches	
" "	—	
9.5 pm "	no men wounded	
" "	Operation order mark II issued	
5.5 am 9.50pm	6 "B" Company in trenches —	
	Operation order mark II sent up	
10 pm "	9 "B" Company to take over relief of 6th Battn	
	Northern relief from 5th Div 12th Brigade	
	Had operations to entrench No III read	
	successful	
10 April TOGETHER	"A" "B" Companies in trenches. No men killed	
	no men wounded.	
	"A" "B" Co in trenches	

Instructions regarding War Diaries and Intelligence Summaries are contained in F. S. Regs., Part II. and the Staff Manual respectively. Title pages will be prepared in manuscript.

WAR DIARY
or
~~INTELLIGENCE SUMMARY~~
(Erase heading not required.)

Army Form C. 2118.

Hour, Date, Place	Summary of Events and Information	Remarks and references to Appendices
12th April 1915 PLOEGSTEERT NOON	"A" + "B" Companies in trenches Lieut A. R. NEWTON-KING seriously wounded and died about 5 hours later. Communication trench established from MONMOUTH-ESSEX trench on our right	[illegible]
13th April 1915 1 PM	A + B Companies in trenches. C + D Companies relieved A + B Coys. detail of reliefs attached which was completed in [illegible] [illegible] [illegible] [illegible] the reliefs were carried out [illegible] [illegible] from [illegible] post platoon [illegible] [illegible] about [illegible] yds from trenches) [illegible] last platoon [illegible] [illegible] billets —	[illegible] Appendix IX
14th April 1915	[illegible] in ~~[illegible]~~ trenches — [illegible] men wounded — C + D Coys in trenches	[illegible] [illegible]

1247 W 3299 200,000 (E) 8/14 J.B.C. & A. Forms/C. 2118/11.

Army Form C. 2118.

WAR DIARY
or
INTELLIGENCE SUMMARY
(Erase heading not required.)

Instructions regarding War Diaries and Intelligence Summaries are contained in F. S. Regs, Part II. and the Staff Manual respectively. Title pages will be prepared in manuscript.

Hour, Date, Place	Summary of Events and Information	Remarks and references to Appendices
April 15. PLOEGSTEERT	A & B Coys in trenches	A
	C & D Coys in trenches at rear, kept in reserve	
10 AM	C & D Coys moved to new huts at OOSTHOVE FARM. Bn. Hd Qrs remained at PLOEGSTEERT.	
7 PM	A & B Coys relieved in trenches by H.4 GLOUCESTER REGT.	A
		in appx VI
	C & D Coys to new billets at OOSTHOVE FARM	
2 PM 16. 4.15	A & B Coys to trenches in relief of 2 MONMOUTHS in the communication trenches have extended. The huts and it so cleared out no long left (?)	
12 PM	Quiet, no enemy shell dropped into ---	
	The new trenches went much lower in front raised. Being occupied -- NORTH of the WARNAVE River	

1247 W 3299 200,000 (E) 8/14 J.B.C. & A. Forms/C. 2118/11.

WAR DIARY
or
INTELLIGENCE SUMMARY
(Erase heading not required.)

Army Form C. 2118.

Hour, Date, Place	Summary of Events and Information	Remarks and references to Appendices
19 April 1915. PLOEGSTEERT	"B" Coy in trenches North of the WARNAVE. "A" Coy in support. Machine gun sergt killed	9/7
20 " "	"B" Coy in trenches A Coy in support. 1 man killed	9/7
21 " "	" "	9/7
2 PM " "	C & D Coys relieved A & B Coys. "D" Coy in front trench. "C" Coy in support. 3 men wounded.	9/7
23. 4. 15	"D" Coy in front trench "C" Coy in support.	9/7
24. 4. 15	" " 3 men wounded	9/7
25. 4. 15	" "	9/7
2 PM 26. 4. 15	A Coy to front trench in relief of D Company. B Coy in support " " C "	9/7

Army Form C. 2118.

WAR DIARY
or
INTELLIGENCE SUMMARY

(Erase heading not required.)

Instructions regarding War Diaries and Intelligence Summaries are contained in F. S. Regs., Part II. and the Staff Manual respectively. Title pages will be prepared in manuscript.

Hour, Date, Place	Summary of Events and Information	Remarks and references to Appendices
27 April 1915 PLOEGSTEERT	A Coy in front trench. B Company in support. Others at rest, scarce.	N
8.30 am		
28 April 1915	A Coy in front trench. B Company in support. Numbers killed.	N
1.30 pm 28/4/15	Intense artillery & rifle fire —	N
4 pm	Coys relieved from trenches.	
1915	Battalion marched from billets to OOSTHOVE FARM near LE NIEPPE.	N
9.30 pm 29.4.15 FALUEUL	Battalion arrived and commenced ? during night.	N
9.5 P.M. 30.4.15	March to ruins of VLAMERTINGHE. Arrived at bivouac.	N
1 PM		
5.30 PM	March by remains of YPRES and across the YSER canal by pontoon bridge to remains	N

Army Form C. 2118.

WAR DIARY
or
INTELLIGENCE SUMMARY

(Erase heading not required.)

Instructions regarding War Diaries and Intelligence Summaries are contained in F. S. Regs., Part II. and the Staff Manual respectively. Title pages will be prepared in manuscript.

Hour, Date, Place	Summary of Events and Information	Remarks and references to Appendices
30/4/15. In BIVOUAC	9 in BIVOUAC. all companies to support trenches in relief of R.W. Kents. Heavy artillery firing heavy attack on the night. 1 man wounded. Trenches very heavily shelled during the night. Also Bois de the	

S E C R E T.  Copy No. 5.

12th Brigade Operation Order.

8-4-1915.

1. The 12th Infantry Brigade will explode a mine tomorrow under the enemy's defences at LE TOUQUET.
   No Infantry attack will be made.

2. In order to cause the enemy to expect an attack and man his trenches previous to the explosion
   (I) Gaps will be made tonight in our wire in front of the trench just East of PACKENHAM'S FARM.
   (II) The Artillery will bombard the trenches and houses in neighbourhood of LE TOUQUET under arrangements to be made by Lieut-Colonel Ross Johnson.
   (III) The Infantry in the trenches from the Railway Barricade southwards to CARTERS FARM will open burst of fire.
   (IV) The trench mortars will bomb Estaminet House and School House.

3. Directly the mine has exploded
   (I) The Artillery will fire on the enemy's lines of approach leading to LE TOUQUET.
   (II) The Infantry will cheer and open heavy burst of fire on the building held by the enemy, and on his communication trenches.

4. Before the explosion, the Infantry must be withdrawn from the two front "SNIPERS HOUSES".

5. A Time Table is attached.

6. Brigade Report Centre at LE BIZEE as usual.

Captain,
Brigade Major, 12th Infantry Brigade.

Issued at 9/15. p.m.

Copy to 14th Brigade R.F.A.
to 2nd Lan: Fus:
to 5th South Lancs.
to 2nd Essex.
to 2nd R.Irish Regt.
to 1st King's Own.
to 2nd Monmouths.
to 4th Division.
to G.O.C., S.M.Bde.
to Bucks Battn., S.M.Div.
Filed.

PROGRAMME.

Time.	Unit.	Objective.
X - 30 minutes. to X - 10 minutes.	**Artillery.** 18 Pr.	Register and fire on trenches behind German Machine Gun House.
	5" Hows.	Register and fire on School House and Pond House.
	Infantry.	Bursts of fire on Houses and Trenches in their front.
	Trench morter.	Fire on Estaminet House and School House.
X - 10 minutes to X	**Artillery.**	No firing.
	Infantry.	Bursts of fire on Houses and Trenches in their front.
	Trench Morter.	No firing.
X -		Mine explodes.
After X	**Artillery** 18 Pdr.	Fire on fire and communication trenches behind Machine Gun House.
	5" Hows.	Fire on School House and Pond House and road between the two.
	Infantry.	Cheer - Bursts of fire on Houses and Trench in their front and on communication trenches.

Note :- The hour 'X' has not yet been decided. All units will be informed by wire.
Watches to be checked at the Brigade Office at 6.a.m.

2nd Bn. The Royal Irish Regiment.

Appendix IV

TRENCH RELIEFS. 13/4/1915.

Number of Relief.	Time of parade at billets.	Unit.	Place.
First.	7. P.M.	No. 12 Platoon.	Burnt-out Farm and further end New Advance Trench.
Second.	7.30 P.M.	No. 9 Platoon.	Advanced Trench.
Third.	7.45 P.M.	No. 10 Platoon.	Near end New Advance Trench.
Fourth.	8.0 P.M.	No. 13 Platoon.	Far end of Convent Trench.
Fifth.	8.15 P.M.	No. 11 Platoon.	Coy. Hd. Qrs. and Reserve Trench.
Sixth.	8.30 P.M.	No. 14 Platoon.	Near end of Convent Trench.

SUPPORTS:-

No. 15 & 16 Platoons will parade at 7.10 P.M., proceed to their allotted places and perform necessary fatigues.

The Machine Gun Section will parade with the Platoon whose trenches they will occupy. The Machine Gun Section will be under the orders of the O.C. "C" Coy.

The O.C. "C" Company will direct and regulate platoons entering and leaving the trenches, and issue such orders as will avoid congestion.

No. 14 Platoon will not advance beyond East Lancashire Support Farm until the first relieved platoon passes that point.

Platoon Commanders will be in front of their platoons when entering the trenches and in rear when leaving.

Platoons in support, when engaged on fatigues conveying rations, etc, should not be allowed to straggle, but kept closed up. In the event of any alarm, material and rations will be piled, and the party will move as quickly as possible to their allotted stations.

Platoon Commanders will report to Battalion Head Quarters' (Lawrence Farm) prior to moving into trenches or into billets, in addition to any reports rendered to their Company Commanders.

Supports will be at Lawrence Farm during daylight and at East Lancashire Support Farm during the hours of darkness.

Lieutenant,

Adjutant, 2nd Bn. The Royal Irish Regiment.

R. Irish (5) G.94

1. The Brigade will be relieved tomorrow.
   The Essex, the East Lancs and the Lan: Fus: will be prepared to march tomorrow morning 28th instant.
   The remaining Battalions will be relieved during the course of the day (28th).
   All trench stores will be handed over to relieving Battalions.
   1st and 2n Line transport will accompany Battalions on the march.

2. All suplus stores will be placed in the storehouse at ARMENTIERES.
   Further details will be forwarded as soon as received.

Acknowledge

12th Brigade.
27-4-1915.

Captain,
Brigade Major.

Relief of Bn of WARNAVE
Appendix II

[Stamp: 12TH INFANTRY BRIGADE, G.75, 16 APR. 1915]

REARRANGEMENT of 10th BRIGADE LINE.

Date.
Nights of.

17/18th.   South Midland Division relieve Royal Irish Regt. in trenches.

18/19th.   Royal Irish Regt. take over from WARNAVE Southwards, relieving three platoons of 2nd Monmouths.

The Royal Irish Regt will also be responsible for garrison (2 platoons) of the new post immediately in rear of above line, and for LONDON FARM (2 Platoons).

19/20th.   2nd Monmouths take over back the trench on the right of their line recently handed over to King's Own and Lanc. Fus.

Arrangements for the above will be made direct between Battalions.

10th Brigade.
16-4-1915.

Captain,
Brigade Major.

4th Div.
12th Inf.Bde.

WAR DIARY

2ND BATTN. THE ROYAL IRISH REGT.

M A Y

1 9 1 5.

74th Bde
28th Div
of R. Irish Regt

Feb.
Vol XII

2 R IRISH
REGIMENT

To go to IV Division

11th Brigade.

Army Form C. 2118.

WAR DIARY
or
INTELLIGENCE SUMMARY
(Erase heading not required.)

Instructions regarding War Diaries and Intelligence Summaries are contained in F. S. Regs., Part II. and the Staff Manual respectively. Title pages will be prepared in manuscript.

Hour, Date, Place	Summary of Events and Information	Remarks and references to Appendices
1st May. Trenches.	Comparatively quiet day. Capt. J.D. Murrough and Lieut. W.P. Hinton wounded, and 16 other casualties.	regret
2nd " "	Quiet day. 7 casualties. Reinforcements of 39 N.C.O. and men joined.	regret
4.30pm 3rd "	Enemy employed Gas Support trenches heavily shelled. Some of our men were gassed, but not badly. Our line unchanged. 8 casualties.	regret
11.30 a.m. 4th "	A report received that enemy appeared to be massing on our front, with signs of attacking our line by Small Leinster Regt. immediately in front of "D" Coy Support trenches, and we were to join outpost. Attack did not develop. 4 casualties.	regret
5th "	Quiet day. Lieut. A.C.B. Stopford wounded. 3 other casualties.	regret

WAR DIARY or INTELLIGENCE SUMMARY

Army Form C. 2118.

(Erase heading not required.)

Instructions regarding War Diaries and Intelligence Summaries are contained in F. S. Regs., Part II, and the Staff Manual respectively. Title pages will be prepared in manuscript.

Hour, Date, Place	Summary of Events and Information	Remarks and references to Appendices
6. May. Trenches	"B" Coy are working party bury twenty shells, 17 Cavalier	93rd...
7. "	Quiet day except for shelling. Lieut. R.C. Anderson wounded, and 12 other casualties.	23rd...
9am 8th "	Heavy bombardment of our positions. Fresh impressions made to meet possible attack from direction of Mouse Farm (later re-named "Shell Trap Farm"). Shells dropped 3' + 6' deep to their right. "B" Coy move to line Wielje and to north of it. "D" Coy to support in prolongation line 3 Mouse line also. Heavy shelling until the evening. Capt. R.C. Watkins, Lieut Bogan attacked; reported missing. Lieut Reeve, Page & S. Frankland (Brig Sig. O.), & T. Huntington, 32., wounded; some other casualties	23rd...
		A 6 p.m. 1.
9. "	Relieve Somerset Regt. on line N.E. of Shell Trap Farm before dawn. Very heavy shelling, which was continued until the evening, but a very trying time. Lieuts. E. L. Livingstone and Ayr. Scratton, R. to M.C., Reeed Evans. Lt. Ramsey also wounded. 56 other casualties.	23rd... "
9.15am "		
am 10th "	Battn. relieved by Rifle Brigade. Marched to Mon. Brilen, about 1 1/2	23rd...

Army Form C. 2118.

WAR DIARY
of
INTELLIGENCE SUMMARY
(Erase heading not required.)

Instructions regarding War Diaries and Intelligence Summaries are contained in F. S. Regs., Part II. and the Staff Manual respectively. Title pages will be prepared in manuscript.

Hour, Date, Place	Summary of Events and Information	Remarks and references to Appendices
4 am 10th May Ref. B23235	Miles N.E. of Poperinghe.	7gth
" 11th "	Resting	7gth
" 12th "	Resting	7gth
8.30am 13th "	Received orders to move at once to 7357 C7807, where we stopped in dug-outs on road until evening	7gth
9 pm "	Moved to trenches and relieved the Rifle Brigade in trenches N.E. of Shell trap farm	Offx 1 ugon
9.30am 14th "	Inniskillins	Received report that about 3 platoons of Reg. leaving Shell trap farm had surrendered to enemy, the enemy and ours remain in farm, and as soon as we came up, we enfiladed by 3 platoons of South Lancashire Regs (T) find they got dispersed slightly wounded, and 14 other casualties.	7gth
" 15th "	Quiet day. 8 casualties	7gth

Army Form C. 2118.

WAR DIARY
~~INTELLIGENCE SUMMARY~~
(Erase heading not required.)

Instructions regarding War Diaries and Intelligence Summaries are contained in F. S. Regs., Part II. and the Staff Manual respectively. Title pages will be prepared in manuscript.

Hour, Date, Place	Summary of Events and Information	Remarks and references to Appendices
1 am 16th May. London	Relieved by Canadian troops, and marched to Château Nameu Brughli, where we bivouacked	17th
2 pm 17th " Château	[Marched] to Eau Buech (1/2 miles) N E of Poperinghe.	17th
18th " " Res Billets	Resting	18th
19th " " "	Resting	19th
20th " " "	Resting	20th

Army Form C. 2118.

WAR DIARY
or
INTELLIGENCE SUMMARY

(Erase heading not required.)

Instructions regarding War Diaries and Intelligence Summaries are contained in F. S. Regs., Part II. and the Staff Manual respectively. Title pages will be prepared in manuscript.

Hour, Date, Place	Summary of Events and Information	Remarks and references to Appendices
11.30 a.m. 21st May 1915.	Marched from Lillers	
1 p.m. " Vlamertinghe	Arrived Chateau, had dinner and tea.	Appx 1
8 p.m. " "	Marched.	Appx 2
10 p.m. " Yser Canal	Arrived, and bivouacked on East Bank.	
9 p.m. 22nd "	Marched to trenches, and took over line as for map. Appx.	Appx. 2
" "	2. from 1st Hants Regt.	Appx 2.
23rd May, trenches	A quiet day, nothing of note necessary.	
1 a.m. 24th " Ind Farm	A bombardment of Turks. Salveny and Energy, and S.2 other	Appx 2
	works going on but did not prove to intense.	Appx 1
3 a.m. " trenches	Battn. stood to arms.	
6.20 a.m. " "	The enemy, favoured by Jpr. attacks. A mass wind blowing	Appx 2.
	from the North-East brought the full volume of the gas	
	on that part of the line occupied by the Bath. Allowing	
	every ask tightening the use of Respirators and keeping	Appx 2.

WAR DIARY or INTELLIGENCE SUMMARY

Army Form C. 2118.

(Erase heading not required.)

Instructions regarding War Diaries and Intelligence Summaries are contained in F. S. Regs., Part II. and the Staff Manual respectively. Title pages will be prepared in manuscript.

Hour, Date, Place	Summary of Events and Information	Remarks and references to Appendices
24th May 1915. Lunette	were taking many of all ranks were overcome by gas. Shell Trap Farm, which had been held by 2 platoons of the 2nd Bn. Roy. Dublin Fusrs, was rushed by the enemy, that enabling them to enfilade our positions of the Blue, which they were then now bombing us with hand grenades. The enemy had our trenches down as far as the height of the "Kemp turn," and our men of our Battn. now being left there the attack was allotted, the enemy loosing the ground to lose between two platoons of "A" Company, under the command of Lieut M. Hay, in the Fortnoys Dugouts, who were in outpost at point "A" on map. These men under the following morning. Our casualties were 17 Officers and 378 other ranks. After what remained of the Battn, were relieved by Royal Scots, Major Chandos and ammunition from Brigade Headquarters this party bivouacks at La Brague for the night.	App II. App: 2 App II. App II. App: 2 App: 3 App II.
6 pm " Liot Farm		
3 pm 25th May 1915 La Brague	Lieut M. Hay, who was the only Officer left of those who two earlier to the trenches, proceeded with the 2 platoons who during the enemy effective Officer remaining, was ordered by the Brigade to take command of the Battn.	App: 3 App II.

Army Form C. 2118.

WAR DIARY
or
INTELLIGENCE SUMMARY
(Erase heading not required.)

Instructions regarding War Diaries and Intelligence Summaries are contained in F. S. Regs., Part II. and the Staff Manual respectively. Title pages will be prepared in manuscript.

Hour, Date, Place	Summary of Events and Information	Remarks and references to Appendices
4 pm 25th May 1915. La Brigue	Battn. marched to Yser Canal.	
" " Yser Canal	Bivouacked on East bank between Nos. 3 and 3a. Bridges.	
" 26th "	Nothing of importance occurred.	WT
" 27th "	Reinforcement of 23 N.C.O. & men joined	WT
" 28th "	Nothing of importance occurred.	WT
" 29th "	Reinforcement of 73 N.C.O. & men joined	WT
" 30th "	Nothing of importance occurred.	WT
" 31st "	Lieuts. Taylor & Hegarty, and 2nd Lieuts. Slon & Hennessy joined	WT

2nd Bn. The Royal Irish Regiment.

APPENDIX. (3)

OFFICERS-CASUALTIES, 24th May, 1915.

Rank and Name.			Unit.	Nature of casualty.
Lt. Col.	Moriarty	R. G. S.	R. I. Regt.	Missing.
Capt.	O'Callaghan	G. A.	,,	Died- Gas Poisoning.
,,	Christie	J. H.	,,	Killed.
,,	Hanly	E. D.	R. Inns.Fus.	Missing.
,,	Pargiter	A. P.	R. I. Regt.	Hospital- Gassed.
Lieut.	Berry	W. H. S.	R. Inns. Fus.	Died-Wounds and gas.
,,	Glascott	J.	N. Staff.Rgt.	Hospital- Gassed.
Lt.& Adj.	Fitzpatrick	T. W.	R. I. Regt.	Hospital- Gassed.
Lieut.	Simpson	V. E.	,,	Hospital- Gassed.
,,	Luckett	J. S.	,,	Died- Gas poisoning.
,,	McLoughlin	J. P.	R. D. Fus.	Hospital- Gassed. Died 25/5/15.
,,	MacSweeney	M. C.	,,	Missing. Unofficially reported in Hospital, England.
,,	Pim	A. S.	R. I. Regt.	Missing. Unofficially reported in Hospital, England.
,,	Crawford	E.	R. Inns.Fus.	Missing. Unofficially reported dead.
2/Lieut.	Maguire	W. R.	Conn. Rangers.	Missing.
,,	Fairbairn	A. H.	R. I. Regt.	Missing.
Lieut.	Magill	R.	R. D. Fus.	Hospital- Gassed.

379 N. C. Os and men casualties.

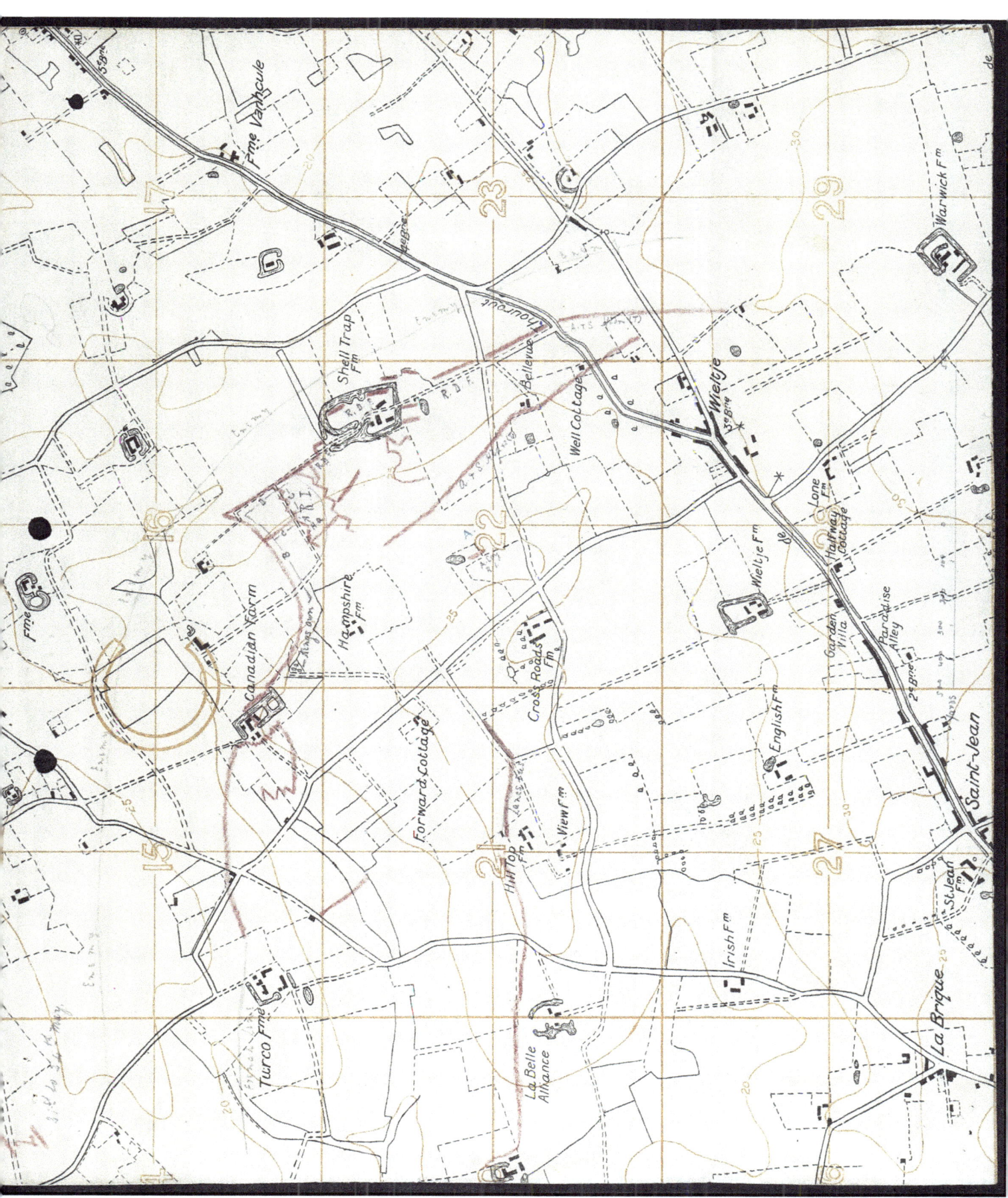

4th Div.
12th Inf.Bde.

WAR DIARY

2ND BATTN. THE ROYAL IRISH REGT.

J U N E

1 9 1 5

WAR DIARY
INTELLIGENCE SUMMARY
(Erase heading not required.)

Army Form C. 2118.

Instructions regarding War Diaries and Intelligence Summaries are contained in F. S. Regs., Part II. and the Staff Manual respectively. Title pages will be prepared in manuscript.

Hour, Date, Place			Summary of Events and Information	Remarks and references to Appendices
9pm	1st Jan. 1915	Yser Canal	Marched to Rue Mellets 1½ Miles N.E. of Poperinghe	seen
	2nd	Rest Billets	Resting	seen
	3rd	"	"	seen
	4th	"	"	seen
	5th	"	Lieut. J.A. Hall, Hon. A. O. Lowe, South Stafford Regt. and 99 R.C.O. men joined	seen
2pm	6th	"	Capt. J.L. Montlu joined and took over command	seen
	7th	Yser Canal	Marched to Yser Canal and bivouacked in dug-outs	seen
	8th	"	Trench digging etc. as night	seen
	9th	"	"	seen
	10th	"	"	seen
	11th	"	"	Lieut. W. Lofthouse joined	seen
	12th	"	"	seen
	13th	"	"	50 R.C.O. men joined	seen
	14th	"	"	seen
	15th	"	"	Capt Lyons joined & Tooke over command	seen
	16th	"	"	seen
	17th	"	"	17 NCOs men joined also Capt JORDAN RALPH Lieut LOWE, Lieut Teague McGRATH	seen
	18th	"	"	Re J.J. Milner Lt Col. Commanding 2/Royal Dub. Fus.	seen

Army Form C. 2118.

WAR DIARY
or
INTELLIGENCE SUMMARY

(Erase heading not required.)

Instructions regarding War Diaries and Intelligence Summaries are contained in F. S. Regs., Part II. and the Staff Manual respectively. Title pages will be prepared in manuscript.

Hour, Date, Place	Summary of Events and Information	Remarks and references to Appendices
June 1915 YSER CANAL 19th 1915	Trench digging &c. at night. Capt Irwin Pemberton, Capt Gurney & 3 shrunt Parties joined	3pm
20th "	"	3pm
21st "		3pm
22nd "		3pm
23rd "	Major Graham joined & took over command	3pm
24th "		3pm
25th "		3pm
26th "	Lieut Crum, Lieut O'Reilly joined to tendere & in a draft of 119 N.C.O's & men	3pm
27th "		3pm
28th "		3pm
29th "		3pm
30th "		3pm

R.H. Kewer
Lieut-Col
Comdg 2/2nd Royal Irish Regt

4th Div.
12th Inf.Bde.

WAR DIARY

2ND BATTN. THE ROYAL IRISH REGT.

JULY

1915.

Army Form C. 2118.

WAR DIARY
or
INTELLIGENCE SUMMARY
(Erase heading not required.)

Instructions regarding War Diaries and Intelligence Summaries are contained in F. S. Regs., Part II. and the Staff Manual respectively. Title pages will be prepared in manuscript.

Hour, Date, Place			Summary of Events and Information	Remarks and references to Appendices
July 1st	YSER CANAL		In dug outs along Canal bank	78ediv 28ediv
"	2nd	"		78ediv
"	3rd	"	7 pm	Received message that Battn would presently proceed to CHATEAU TROIS TOURS (nr BOESINGHE) the following night 4th	App. I
"	3rd	"	7 pm	Received message for Brigade that enemy were using gas shells, no serious result through 9th who were complaining of being sore eyed for some time.	App. II
"	"	"	8 pm	Received message from 1/6th W. Yorks. that they were relieving us. Their advance parties 3 other ranks + 124 men arrived at - hour. Transport, ink, stores etc. arrived to Canal.	App. IV
"	4th	"		Received scattered information from Brigade re move.	App. III
"	"	"	9.15 pm	(1st Company (D)) Left the Canal bank for CHATEAU TROIS TOURS.	78ediv
"	5th	CHATEAU TROIS TOURS		In wood around CHATEAU TROIS TOURS	78ediv 28ediv
"	6th	"			Appendix V
"	"	"		Received orders that Battalion moved proceed to PROVEN the next night with the remainder of 12th Bgde.	28ediv
"	7th	"	11.30 pm	The Battalion left CHATEAU TROIS TOURS for PROVEN by 8th Wore Yorks.	28ediv
"	8th	"	about 6 am	Arrived at billets near PROVEN. Genl PLUMMER and Battalion at - and Transport.	78ediv

Lo Sf Cluse Lt Col
Comdg 5/ The Royal Irish Regt

1247 W 3299 200,000 (E) 8/14 J.B.C. & A. Forms/C. 2118/11.

Army Form C. 2118.

WAR DIARY
or
INTELLIGENCE SUMMARY

(Erase heading not required.)

Instructions regarding War Diaries and Intelligence Summaries are contained in F. S. Regs., Part II. and the Staff Manual respectively. Title pages will be prepared in manuscript.

Hour, Date, Place		Summary of Events and Information	Remarks and references to Appendices
July 9th	PROVEN	Billeted in farms near PROVEN	7gpm
" 10th	" 6.15pm	" Received message from Brigade that the Battalion was to proceed to St JANS CAPELL with 5th Bn 6th CORPS	app VI 7gpm. 7gpm.
" 11th	"	"	7gpm.
" 12th	"	Billeting Party sent to St JANS CAPELL ahead to MQ 50th DIV	9gpm.
" 13th	" 8.15am	Commenced march to St JANS CAPELL near BAILLEUL	7gpm.
St JANS CAPELL	1.30pm	Arrived at St JANS CAPELL & billeted in farms	9.8pm.
" 14th	St JANS CAPELL	In billets near St JANS CAPELL	
" 15th	"	"	
" 16th	"	"	
" 17th	"	"	
" 18th	"	"	Received message that Battn was to proceed	
" 19th	"	to GODVERSVELDE and entrain there at 3.33am July 20th	app VII

E. St Michel Lieut Col
Cmdy 5/7th Royal Scots Regt

Army Form C. 2118.

WAR DIARY
or
INTELLIGENCE SUMMARY

(Erase heading not required.)

Instructions regarding War Diaries and Intelligence Summaries are contained in F. S. Regs., Part II. and the Staff Manual respectively. Title pages will be prepared in manuscript.

Hour, Date, Place			Summary of Events and Information	Remarks and references to Appendices
July 20th	ST JANS CAPELL		In billets near ST JANS CAPELL	18
" 21st	"		Received orders to send billeting party to FRESCHVILLERS also 4 Div orders for entraining & detraining	App VIII, IX, X & XI 18
		8.45pm	Left ST JANS CAPELL	18
" 22nd	GODVERSVELDE	11.30pm	Arrived at GODVERSVELDE	18
"	"	12.30am	Entrained at "	18
" 22nd	TRAIN	9.30am	Arrived at DOULLENS where the Battn detrained & marched to a field at FRESCHVILLERS 2 miles from DOULLENS	18
" 23rd	FRESCHVILLERS	3pm	Left FRESCHVILLERS & marched to billets at LOUVENCOURT	18
" 23rd	LOUVENCOURT		In Billets	18
" 24 "	"		"	18
" 25 "	"	10am	Inspection by G.O.C. 3rd Army – General Munro	18
" 26 "	"		"	18
" 27 "	"		"	18
" 28 "	"		"	18
" 29 "	ACHEUX	10am	The Battalion marched to ACHEUX. In Billets in the town. Draft of 9 NCOs and men arrived	App 19
" 30 "	ACHEUX		In Billets. Draft of 164 NCOs and men arrived	19
" 31 "	"		"	18

E. A. Pope Lieut-Col
Comdg 2/The Royal Scots Regt.

"A" Form. Appendix I   Army Form C.2121
MESSAGES AND SIGNALS.

TO O. Tank
    4th RW

Sender's Number: Rm 84   Day of Month: 3rd   AAA

~~You will~~

Your Battalion will probably proceed to TROIS TOURS tomorrow evening aaa. You should send a billeting party of one officer and 5 men to report to 4th RW HQ by 2 pm to find out where your Bn will be located.

From: 17th Bde
Place:
Time: 1.53 pm

"A" Form. Appendix II   Army Form C. 2121.
MESSAGES AND SIGNALS.

TO   R. Firth

Sender's Number: BM59   Day of Month: 3   AAA

Reported that enemy are using gas shells to the west of 12th Bde lines. A

Appendix II War Diary.

Appendix III

12th Brigade No. B.M. 76

Royal Irish.
----

1. Your Battalion will go into Bivouac tonight in the grounds at Chateau des Trois Tours B.28.
   Cross Canal by No. 6 Bridge and march across country to BRIELEN. An officer to meet the Staff Captain at Brigade H.Q. at 2.p.m. to reconnoitre the route.

2. The Machine Gun now in front trench will remain there.

3. You should send an orderly to your transport to order what vehicles you require. These vehicles will come by Cross Roads B.29.d. but are not to cross that point till 10.p.m. Machine Guns etc, with as small a party as possible, will be left on West bank at No. 5 Bridge till the transport arrives. The Transport will return to Trois Tours by the Road.

4. You will be required to find carrying parties totalling 150 men tonight parading at 9-10.p.m. These parties can return independently via the road to Trois Tours. The packs etc. of these men can be left with the Machine Guns at No. 5 Bridge until their return.

5. You will probably stay at Trois Tours till the evening of the 7th.

6. Your guards on bridges will be relieved by 6th West Yorks about 10-30.p.m. You can make any arrangements you like for their move to Trois Tours after relief.

   Acknowledge.

12th Brigade.
4-7-1915.

Major,
Brigade Major.

"A" Form Appendix IV. Army Form C. 2121.
MESSAGES AND SIGNALS.   No. of Message

Prefix	Code	m.	Words	Charge	This message is on a/c of:	Recd. at	m.
Office of Origin and Service Instructions.			Sent		Service.	Date	
			At	n.		From	
			To			By	
			By		(Signature of "Franking Officer.")		

TO Adjt. Royal Irish Regt.

Sender's Number.	Day of Month	In reply to Number	AAA
	Third		

The 12th Brigade have been asked to request you to send Guides to ASYLUM, YPRES for us to morrow night AAA with regard to the transport could you inform me whether we will be able to bring down a wagon or so to our dug outs on the canal bank to morrow night or to some place where we can get at what we want, men which cannot be carried by to Rhine drivers, officers kits etc — We would not bring any transport with the men but leave instructions for it to come on afterwards. Say about 11 PM.

From Adjt 1/Bn W. Yorkshire Regt.
Place
Time

The above may be forwarded as now corrected.   (Z)   G P McKenna Capt Adjt
P.10   Censor.   Signature of Addressor or person authorised to telegraph in his name

P.T.O.

Appendix F

SECRET.   12th Brigade Operation Order No. 2.   Copy No. 2

6-7-1915.

1. The Brigade will be relieved tomorrow night 7/8th and will move to PROVEN area according to attached Time Table.

2. Battalion relieving Essex will cross by No. 4 Bridge at 9-30.p.m. South Lancs and King's Own at 10.p.m. Officer Commanding 6th West Yorks will send an officer to King's Own H.Q. tomorrow morning to arrange for relief of Left Company of King's Own.
The 6th West Yorks Company will not leave the Canal Bank till 9-30.p.m. and will move via road leading from No. 5 Bridge.

3. Guides will be sent to No. 4 Bridge, West Bank as shown on attached table No. 2 by 9.p.m.

4. On relief Battalions should march independently by Companies via No. 4 Bridge to their half way rest places. On leaving their rest places in afternoon Battalions will march by parties not larger than Companies. Officers Commanding King's Own and South Lancs will arrange at what hour their Battalions march off. Officer Commanding Essex will ascertain this hour and arrange that his Battalion is clear of the roads.

5. First Line transport,(other than that required at Canal Bank) and Baggage Wagons will join Battalions (except Royal Irish) at their half way billets. Transport for Royal Irish will join Unit on march.
The above under Regimental arrangements.
Transport required on Canal Bank must not xxxxx pass Cross Roads B.29.d.x before 10-15.p.m. and will draw up on road South of No. 4 Bridge. They should be timed to arrive just before they are wanted so as not to be kept waiting.

6. Table 3 shows trench stores etc. that will, or will not be left in trenches. Reference this table all shovels will be left. Regimental establishment will be made up in billets.

Acknowledge.

Major,
6-7-1915.   Brigade Major, 12th Infantry Brigade.

Issued at   p.m.

Copies to King's Own.
Royal Irish.
Lan: Fus:
Essex.
South Lancs.
6th West Yorks.
Brigade Transport Officer.
File.

Appendix V

Table. 1.

Reliefs on night 7/8th July, 1915.

Battalion to be relieved.	Relieving Unit.	Hour.	Halfway Halting places.	Destination. Billeting Areas.
Royal Irish. (2)	8th West Yorks.	10/pm	Go direct after relief.	Marked 4 on map.
Essex. (1)	8th West Yorks.	—	A.21.	Marked 1 on map.
King's Own. (1) left Coy Bn (less 1 Coy)	~~Left Coy.~~ 1 Coy 6th W.Yorks. Bn.(less 1 Coy)7th W.Yorks less 2 Coys.		Wood in A.16.a.	Marked 3 on Map.
Lancs. (1)	2 Coys 7th W.Yorks.		Wood in A.16.a.	Marked 5 on Map.
Lan.Fus. (3)			A.21	Marked 2 on Map.

(1) NOTE.— All Battalions except Royal Irish march from halfway resting place via chemin militaire(not on map)which runs N.W. through wood in A.16.a – crossroads in square A.8.b.10.5 – road Junction A.7.b.9.6 – Convent at St.Siste(A.1.d.) – Cross Roads in W.10.d.9.3. – Cross Roads W.4.d.5.1.– Road Junction at W.3.c.0.9. – Proven.
This road will be marked by piquets of the Divl.squadron.

(2) Royal Irish will march via Poperinghe & Pan de Nooge cabt."

(3) Under arrangements of the 11th Brigade on 9th/10th.

Appendix V Table 3.

4th Div. Q/115.

Trench Stores and Equipment.

A.	B.
Trench Stores (to be handed over in trenches.)	Trench Equipment (to be taken to new trenches.)
Pumps.	Periscopes.
Bailers.	Brigade Reserve Tools.
Loopholed Plates.	Trench Mortars and Ammunition.
Braziers.	Klaxon Horns.
Buckets.	Gongs.
Fixed Rifle Rests.	Very Pistols.
Vermorel Sprayers.	Telescopic Rifles.
Grenades (in the trenches)	Periscopic Rifles.
Very Pistol Lights "	Telephone Instruments.
Tools (other than mobilisation equipment and Brigade reserve).	Bombs, Grenades and Very Lights in Brigade Bomb Stores.
R.E. stores such as — sandbags, wire, metal, felting, tramlines and trollies.	Shot Guns.
	Viscoscopes.
Fire Boxes.	Bomb Bags.
Tins of solution for sprayers.	Wire cutters.
All stores and supplies in Defended Posts.	Poles carrying M.G.
Standards of horns and gongs.	Catapults.
S.A.A. in trenches including all loose bandoliers.	Observers veils.
Water tanks and barrels.	Weather cocks.
Rockets and stands.	Water Jars and Tins.
Syringes 50%	Rifle Rests made by Division.
	Short rifles.
	Wheel and hand barrows.

"A" Form.   Army Form C. 2121.
MESSAGES AND SIGNALS.

Appendix V

To: Royal Irish

Sender's Number: LC 675   Day of Month: 10th   AAA

6th Corps wire begins AAA 2nd corps wish 2nd Royal Irish Regt to join that corps at St Jeans Cappel on the 13th inst. AAA Further instruction will be issued

From: 12th Bde
Time: 6 pm

Lieut

"A" Form. Appendix VII Army Form C. 2121.
MESSAGES AND SIGNALS. No. of Message _____

Prefix ___ Code ___ m.	Words	Charge	This message is on a/c of	Recd. at ___ m.
Office of Origin and Service Instructions.				
	Sent		.... Service.	Date
....	At ___ m.			From
....	To		(Signature of "Franking Officer.")	By
	By			

TO 2nd Royal Irish Regiment

| Sender's Number. | Day of Month | In reply to Number | AAA |
| Q 366 | 19 | — | |

Following received from 4th Division begins
2nd Royal Irish will depart from GODEWAERSVELDE
at 2.33 am on 22nd July AAA They should be
at station 3 hours before departure train AAA
grass field in Q 11 D. 3.1 is available as resting
place for this battalion from noon 21st AAA They
should have current days rations and supply
wagons filled AAA

From 50th Division
Place
Time

"A" Form.

MESSAGES AND SIGNALS.

Appendix VIII

TO ~~Kings Own~~ ~~Lan Fus~~ ~~Essex~~
~~South Lancs~~ ~~R Irish~~

Sender's Number	Day of Month	In reply to Number	
Bm. 236.	21st		AAA

Officers comdg billeting parties of Battns will arrange to meet their Battns at DOULLENS station to lead them to their billets which will be at FRESCHVILLERS except the South Lancs which will be at LOUVENCOURT AAA Trains with Battns arrive as follows at DOULLENS :-
Kings Own   9.45 pm   21st
Lan Fus   12.30 am   22nd
Essex   4.30 am   22nd
R Irish   9.30 am   22nd
South Lancs 1.30 pm   22nd AAA
If possible the R Irish will send billeting party by the Essex train

From ~~having~~ GODEWAERSVELDE at ~~——~~
Place 9.33 pm 21st AAA Copies
Time to Billeting parties except R Irish

Appendix IX

SECRET. 4th Div. Q/639.

Supply Col.,

1. The Fourth Division (less Mechanical Portion of the Divisional Ammunition Column and Motor Ambulances) will entrain at GODEWAERSVELDE and CASSEL commencing on the morning 21st July.

2. A table shewing allocation of units to trains and hours of departure is issued herewith.
   The estimated strength of units in Officers, men, horses and vehicles is entered thereon.
   The MARCHE No. (thus, M.B.7) is the official description of the Train.
   Continental Time is used, e.g. -
Date.	Time of Dep.		
21/7	17.33	=	5.33 p.m. on 21st July.
23/7	4.31	=	4.31 a.m. on 23rd July.

   The RENDEZVOUS prior to entrainment is also given, and units whose times of departures are between 2 and 10 hrs. may bivouac there for the night if desired.

3. Units must arrive at the entraining point 3 clear hours before the time of departure. It is essential that the trains leave up to time.
   Units must note the time allotted for entraining, i.e. the interval that elapses between the departure of their train and that of the previous one.
   The O.C. Train will arrange for sufficient fatigue parties to ensure the train being loaded in time. Ramps will be provided by R.T.O.s.

4. Officers will be on duty as follows:-
   GODEWAERSVELDE - - - Capt. SHELLEY.
   CASSEL - - - - Major LEGGETT.
   DOULLENS - - - - Major SMYTH OSBOURNE *
   MENDICOURT - - - - Capt. LANYON.
   * Will give detail of destination to each train on arrival at DOULLENS

5. Duration of Journey. About 7 hours. Officers i/c Trains will receive a Time Table from R.T.O. at entraining stations. There will be no halt for meals etc.

6. Route. For units entraining at CASSEL,
   "   "   "   GODEWAERSVELDE.
   These will be issued later.

7. Supplies. All units entraining will carry with them the current day's rations. Supply wagons will be full, and will accompany units.

8. Water. Water carts will be entrained full. O.C. Units will ensure that these carts are filled before leaving their present billets. Water for horses will probably be provided in tubs at the entraining stations.

9. Breast ropes. Units will provide breast ropes for all wagons carrying horses.

10. Rendezvous prior to entraining. Units are held responsible that these are left in a sanitary condition.

F. F. READY, Lt.Col.,
A.A. & Q.M.G., 4th Division.

19/7/15.

Composition of train W.B.10.
34 Covered wagons
13 Flat
1 Carriage.

1 Covered wagon taken
40 men,
8 L.D. Horses
6. H.D. "

1 Flat taken
3 — 4 prs wheels.

1360

Appendix X.

Table shewing allocation of units to trains and Hours of Departure.

Ref. sheet 27, $\frac{1}{40,000}$

Place of Entrainment — GODEWAERSVELDE.

Train No. and Marche No.	Date.	Time of Departure.	Name of Unit.	Rendezvous prior to entrainment.	Remarks.
No. 1 W.B. 2	21/7	9.33	12th Bde.H.Q., No.4 Sec.Sig.Co., No. 4 Co.Train, Cable Sec.	Q.11.d 3.1	
No. 2 W.B. 4	21/7	14.45	1st Kings Own	Q.17.b N.W.	
No. 3 W.B. 6	21/7	17.33	2nd Lancs. Fus., Div. Res. Coy.,	Q.17.b S.E.	
No. 4 W.B. 8	21/7	21.33	2nd Essex	Q.18 Central	
No. 5 W.B. 10	22/7	2.33	2nd R.Irish Regt.	Q.11.d 3.1	
No. 6 W.B. 12	22/7	6.33	5th South Lancs.	Q.17.b N.W.	
No. 7 W.B. 14	22/7	9.33	Div.H.Q.,10th Bde. H.Q.,No.2 Sec.Sig. Coy.,No.2 Coy. Train	Q.17.b S.E.	
No. 8 W.B. 16	22/7	14.45	1st R. Warwicks	Q.18 Central	
No. 9 W.B. 18	22/7	17.33	2nd Seaforth Highrs.	Q.11.d 3.1	
No.10 W.B. 20	22/7	21.33	1st R. Irish Fus.	Q.17.b N.W.	
No.11 W.B. 22	23/7	2.33	2nd R.Dub.Fus.	Q.17.b S.E.	
No.12 W.B. 24	23/7	6.33	A. & S. Highrs.	Q.18 Central	
No.13 W.B. 26	23/7	9.33	1st Som. L.I.	Q.11.d 3.1	
No.14 W.B. 28	23/7	14.45	1st East Lancs.	Q.17.b N.W.	
No.15 W.B. 30	23/7	17.33	1st Hants.	Q.17.b S.E.	
No.16 W.B. 32	23/7	21.33	1st Rifle Bde.	Q.18 Central	
No.17 W.B. 34	24/7	2.35	11th Fd.Amb., 128th How.Am.Col.	Q.11.d 3.1	
No.18 W.B. 36	24/7	6.33	10th Fd.Amb. 86th How.Amm.Col.	Q.17.b N.W.	
No.19 W.B. 38	24/7	9.33	½ 5th Sec. Div. Am. Col.	Q.17.b S.E.	
No.20 W.B. 40	24/7	14.45	½ 6th Sec. Div. Am. Col.	Q.18 Central	
No.21 W.B. 42	24/7	17.33	H.Q. Div.Amm.Col. ½ 5th & 6th Secs.	Q.11.d 3.1	

Appendix XI

DETRAINMENT   4th DIVISION.

Unit.	Time of detrainment	Place of detrainment.	1st Billet	2nd Billet	Remarks.
12th Fd. Amb.	3.30 P.M. 21st	Mondicourt	Marieux, 1st Secn. to Freschvillers Marieux	2nd Secn to Betrancourt	Main Station Marieux
22nd Trench How.	3.50 P.M. 21st	Doullens	Freschvillers	Betrancourt	Move evening 22nd Refill between Vaucelles and Louvencourt
12th Brig. H.Q.	4.30 P.M. 21st	"	"	Louvencourt	
No. 4 Co. Train	4.30 P.M. 21st	"	"		
Cable Socn.	4.30 P.M. 21st	Mondicourt	Amplier		
Squadron	8.50 P.M. 21st	"	Acheux		
H.Q. Sig. Co.	8.50 P.M. 21st	Doullens	Freschvillers	Betrancourt	
King's Own Cyclists	9.45 P.M. 21st	Mondicourt	Louvencourt		Refill Sarton
Train H.Q. & No. 1 Co.	11.30 P.M. 21st	"	Sarton		
	11.30 P.M. 21st				
Lancs. Fus.	12.30 a.m. 22nd	Doullens	Freschvillers	Betrancourt	Move evening 22nd
Reserve Co.	12.30 a.m. 22nd	"	"	Acheux	Move evening 22nd
E.Lancs. Fd. Co	2.11 a.m. 22nd	Mondicourt	Thievres		
Sanitary Socn.	2.11 a.m. 22nd	"	"		
Mob. Vet. Secn.	2.11 a.m. 22nd	"	"		
Essex Regt.	4.30 a.m. 22nd	Doullens	Freschvillers	Louvencourt	Move evening 22nd
H.Q. 14th F.A.B.	7.30 a.m. 22nd	Mondicourt	Thievres		
68th Batty.	7.30 a.m. 22nd	Doullens	Freschvillers	Louvencourt	Move evening 22nd
R.Irish Regt.	9.30 a.m. 22nd	Mondicourt	Thievres		via Freschvillers moving thenco in evening 22nd
88th Batty.	11.30 a.m. 22nd	Doullens	Louvencourt		
S.Lancs. Regt.	1.30 p.m. 22nd	Doullens			
88th Batty	3.30 p.m. 22nd	Mondicourt	Thievres	Vauchelles	Move evening 23rd Refill between Vaucelles and Marieux
Div. H.Q.	4.30 p.m. 22nd	Doullens	A cheux	"	
10th Brig. H.Q.	4.30 p.m. 22nd	Doullens	Freschvillers	"	
No. 2 Co. Train	4.30 p.m. 22nd	Doullens	"		
H.Q. 29th F.A.B.	6.50 p.m. 22nd	Mondicourt	Thievres		

2nd R. S. Regt.   Appendix XII

O.C. C Coy   XII

The Battalion will march at 10 am tomorrow (Thursday, 29th inst.) to ACHEUX.
Order of march. HQ. B. C. D. A.
HQ. B. Coy will move off at 10 am from Bn HdQrs., the remaining Coys moving at intervals of 15 mins.
   Reveille 5.0. am.
   Breakfast 7.30 am.
Officers kits will be ready to be loaded at the Transport lines by 9-0 am.
A Billeting party consisting of the Qr. Mr., 2/Lt Newill, 4. C.O.'s & 2 Bgrs. will proceed ahead of Bn. parading at Battn. HQ. Qrs. at 7. am.

Please inform CQMS

F J Rhodes Capt
Act. Adjt. 2nd R S Regt.
11.45 pm 28/7/15

4th Division

2nd. Royal Irish Regt.

Joined from the 12th Bde 26-7-15,

Less September,

August to December
1915

4th Div.
11th Inf. Bde.

WAR DIARY

2ND BATTN. THE ROYAL IRISH REGT.

A U G U S T

1 9 1 5.

(Joined 11th Inf. Bde. 26.7.1915 from 12th Inf. Bde.)

WAR DIARY or INTELLIGENCE SUMMARY

(Erase heading not required.)

Army Form C. 2118.

Instructions regarding War Diaries and Intelligence Summaries are contained in F. S. Regs., Part II. and the Staff Manual respectively. Title pages will be prepared in manuscript.

Hour, Date, Place	Summary of Events and Information	Remarks and references to Appendices
August 1st ACHEUX	In billets	1R
2nd "	"	R
3rd "	"	7½Rm
4th "	"	7½Rm
5th "	"	7½Rm
6th "	Received message Col. Bulli would now be ENGLEBELMAR 6 miles. Draft (8) arrived.	7½Rm Apps XIII
7 am "	moved to out of billets at ACHEUX into new billets at ENGLEBELMAR	28Rm
8th ENGLEBELMAR In billets		7½Rm
9th "		7½Rm
9 pm "	2 Coys went into Trenches A Coy with E.LANCS, B Coy with SOMERSET.LI	
10th "	A + B Coys returned from Trenches. A Coy 5 wounded B Coy nil.	28Rm 28Rm
11th "	"	28Rm
12th "	"	7½Rm
13th "	2 Companies C + D proceeded to Trenches C Coy attached to Rifle Brigade, D Coy to Hampshire Regt.	7½Rm
13th 7.20 pm "	Draft of 30 men arrived	

Army Form C. 2118.

WAR DIARY
or
INTELLIGENCE SUMMARY
(Erase heading not required.)

Instructions regarding War Diaries and Intelligence Summaries are contained in F. S. Regs., Part II. and the Staff Manual respectively. Title pages will be prepared in manuscript.

Hour, Date, Place	Summary of Events and Information	Remarks and references to Appendices
August 14 ENGLEBELMER	In billets (2 coys in Tourelles)	
" 15"	" 2 enemy returned from Tourelles, G Coy to Terailles. D Coy unnumbered.	W. Col.
" 16	In billets. on movement	
" 17"	" Capt D Again (the Worcestershire Reg) arrived and assumed command of Battn. 2nd Lieut E.W. Mitchell invalided to Eng (and	(A. far W.J. DUGAN A.D.O.
" 18"	In Billets. Orders for move to MESNIL issued.	
" 19"	"	
" 20" MESNIL	Battalion moves at 8.30 pm to billets in MESNIL (in Brigade Support)	
" 21"	Brigade Support	
" 22"	do	
" 23"	do	
" 24"	do	
" 25"	do	W. Col.
" 26 "	do	
" 27 " ENGLEBELMER	Battalion A.G. Companies allotted to SYDELINES and 2 Cays temporarily garrisoning trenches	
" 4 trenches	50. 55 inclusive of 4" Insulated line	

WAR DIARY or INTELLIGENCE SUMMARY

Army Form C. 2118.

Hour, Date, Place	Summary of Events and Information	Remarks and references to Appendices
August 26 ENGLEBELMER	B" & "D" Coys relieved trenches 51–85 inclusive. Positions as per attached maps. Regt. has been instructed by the Germans have been constructed by an average 300/350 E of our line. Our junction along the ridge W of BEAUMONT HAMEL is [?]. Their trenches [?] wiring featured of [?]. The construction of bomb-proof [?] can be clearly drawn in the [?] of artillery and on full bomb-proofing of the other [?] which [?] found upon the [?] reed bundles [?] which [?] appears to [?] [?] very traffic [?] [?] [?] very traffic [?] [?] [?] bridges upon hastily [?] [?] [?] on [?] [?] wide [?] above on ENGLEBELMER so C. H.Q. are temporary H.Q. which 2 coys are [?] has always appeared to [?] his [?] [?] [?] 2nd [?] 2 men wounded one [?]	Appendix XIV W.M. W.M. W.M. W.M. W.M.

Strength 31 Aug. '15   29 Officers 1022 O.R.

Appendix XIII

"C" Form (Original).
MESSAGES AND SIGNALS.
Army Form C. 2123.
No. of Message 47

Prefix — Code — Words 86

From 3K
By Lee

Service Instructions: two adds 3K

Office 8.45am Received 8.57am

TO 4th Divn R. Irish.

Sender's Number 69   Day of Month 6th   AAA

The Royal Irish Regt will march to Billets in ENGLEBELMER tomorrow at 7am aaa Companies will move at 10 minutes interval aaa Two telephonists will take over the wires at the present Bde HQ by 12 noon today aaa The 11th Bde office at ENGLEBELMER will close at 12.30 pm today and the 11th Brigade POSTE DE COMMANDEMENT will open at MARTINSART at the same hour aaa addressed R. Irish repld 4th Divn

FROM PLACE & TIME 11th Bde 8.45am

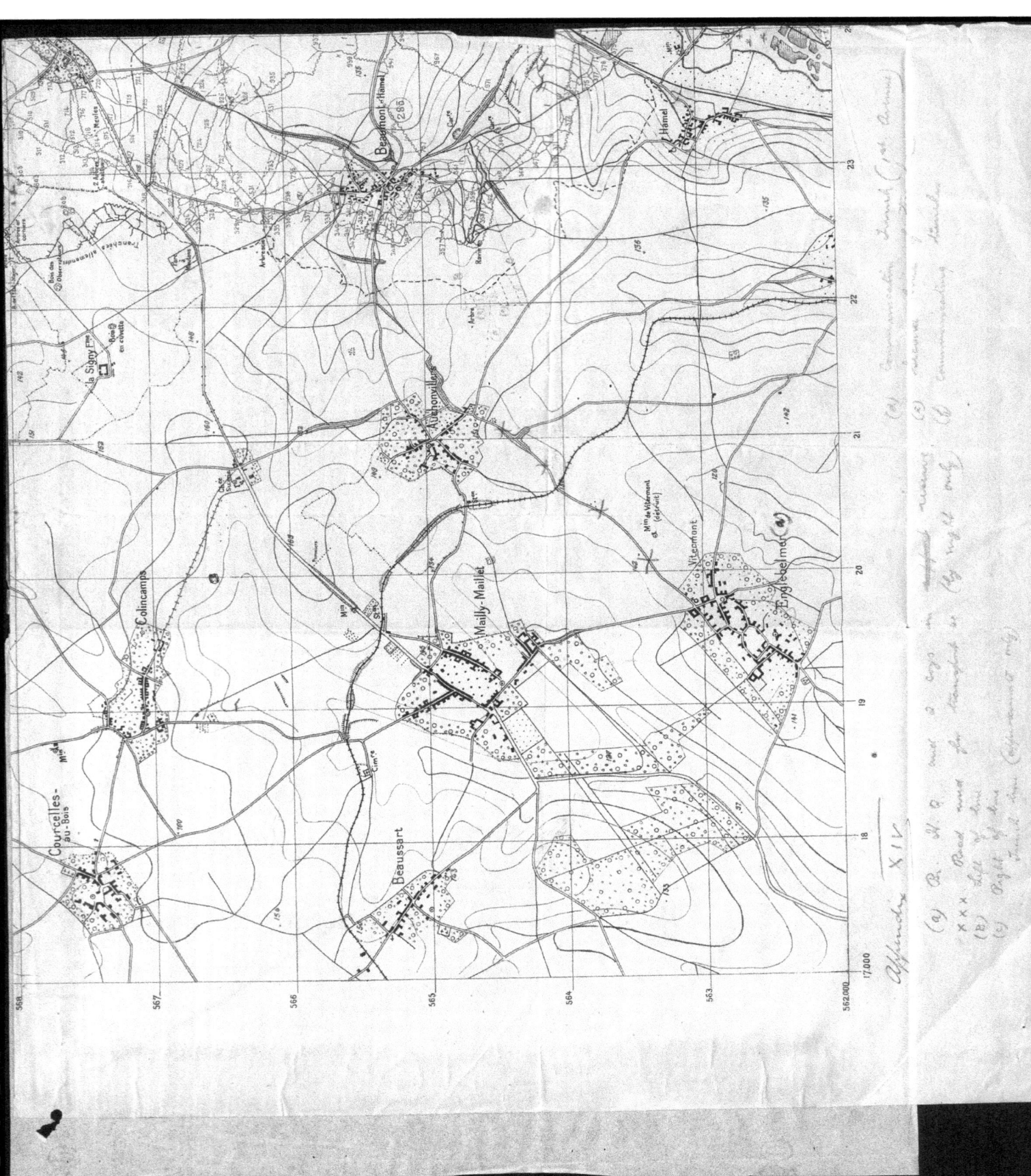

4th Div.
11th Inf. Bde.

WAR DIARY

2ND BATTN. THE ROYAL IRISH REGT.

SEPTEMBER

1 9 1 5.

------ M I S S I N G ------

4th Div.
11th Inf. Bde.

WAR DIARY

2ND BATTN. THE ROYAL IRISH REGT.

OCTOBER

1915.

(Joined 11th Inf. Bde. 26.7.15 from 12th Inf. Bde.)

Army Form C. 2118.

WAR DIARY
or
INTELLIGENCE SUMMARY.
(Erase heading not required.)

October
September 1915.
2nd Batt" The Royal Irish Regt.

Place	Date	Hour	Summary of Events and Information	Remarks and references to Appendices
ENGLEBELMER	1-10-15		Two coys in trenches & 2 coys billeted in ENGLEBELMER, relieving each other weekly, as in September. Usual patrols; enemy very quiet.	
	5		Enemy were hard working on their second line trenches & shelled by our Artillery.	
	7.		Enemy shelled our trenches without effect + no artillery retaliated.	
	8.		Enemy again shelled our trenches, one officer 2nd Lieut-Delamy, being buried in his dug-out and badly bruised.	
	9-11.		All quiet.	
	12.		Our machine guns fired on enemy working party with success, stopping all work.	
	13-14.		All quiet.	
	15.		Captain Slee wounded by a German sniper.	
	16-31		All quiet. During these days considerable work was done in improving our front trenches, shelters, and in completing a new Batt" Headquarters dug-out. Large working parties were also employed to the R.E. for assistance in the building of a trench railway.	

4th Div.
11th Inf.Bde.

WAR DIARY

2ND BATTN. THE ROYAL IRISH REGT.

NOVEMBER

1 9 1 5.

(Joined 11th Inf. Bde. 26.7.15 from 12th Inf. Bde.)

Army Form C. 2118

WAR DIARY
or
INTELLIGENCE SUMMARY.

(Erase heading not required.)

2nd Batt" The Royal Irish Reg

Instructions regarding War Diaries and Intelligence Summaries are contained in F. S. Regs., Part II. and the Staff Manual respectively. Title pages will be prepared in manuscript.

Place	Date 1915	Hour	Summary of Events and Information	Remarks and references to Appendices
ENGLEBELMER	November			
	1-9		Two companies in trenches, two companies in billets; ENGLEBELMER relieving each other as in October. Principal work in trenches; patrolling the line and improving & draining the trenches; building shelters & dug-outs for officers and men.	
	10		Nothing of importance took place. 2nd Lieut Parker-Fitzgerald, 3rd Royal Irish Fusiliers joined the Batt"	
	12		See Appendix I regarding effect of weather on German trenches	
	12-18		Nothing of importance.	
	19		See Appendix II re sounds heard by an patrol in German Trench.	
	21		See Appendix III. re sounds of German mining heard beneath our right sector.	
	22		See Appendix IV re officers patrol. This patrol was congratulated by the B.G.C. 11th Bde	
	23		See Appendix V re report of mining expert on presence of German mine	
	24		Lieut I.W. Fitzpatrick rejoined the Batt". Lieut G.G. Price joined from 4th Batt"	
	25-28		Nothing of importance took place.	
	29		See Appendix VI re officers patrol	
	30		Lieut I.W. Usher, 2nd Lieuts I.F. Perrin, S.C. Grant and A.W. Surgey joined the Batt" from 3rd Batt" Dublin.	

"A" Form. Army Form C. 2121.
MESSAGES AND SIGNALS.

Prefix SP	Code AE	m.	Words 15	Charge	This message is on a/c of	Recd. at 1.33 p m.
Office of Origin and Service Instructions.			Sent		...................Service.	Date 12th
ARE			At m.			From +R1
			To		(Signature of "Franking Officer.")	By Pte Davis

| TO | HQ | | Appendix I | |

| Sender's Number. | Day of Month | In reply to Number | |
| *ari/8 | 12th | | A A A |

afternoon report aaa patrols have nothing to report aaa intelligent aaa enemy very quiet the weather appears to be troubling him as he is working hard repairing the damage caused by heavy rain in the trenches aaa the germans seem to make good use of their communication trenches apparently occupying them only aaa several trenches must be badly flooded as the enemy come out and move along the open despite our fire aaa ~~be hostile 2666 artillery as short~~ ...

From			
Place			
Time			

The above may be forwarded as now corrected. (Z)

Censor. Signature of Addressee or person authorised to telegraph in his name.
* This line should be erased if not required.

"C" Form (Quadruplicate).   Army Form C. 2123 A.

MESSAGES AND SIGNALS.

No. of Message..............

SM ALF
+ M

Charges to Pay   Office Stamp.
£   s.   d.

Service Instructions.

Handed in at the............Office, at............m. Received here at 2.7 m.

TO   H P Appendix II.

| Sender's Number | Day of Month. | In reply to Number. | AAA |
| AR1/2 | 19th | | |

patrols have nothing to report aaa
intelligence aaa ~~much~~ shouting and
laughing and shouts of left right left
right in german followed apparently
by a fight aaa machine gun fire
dispersed german working party at
Ravine ~~en-p~~ at 12.30 am aaa
~~...~~ aaa ~~enemy trenches shelled
and dug at aaa canto proposed aaa
sent..... corrected aaa sentry~~
~~.............. 7.30 2 PM~~
~~Casualty returned absentee aaa~~

FROM   Dlay 4287 cpl Blanche
PLACE   to hospital aaa
TIME

GALE & POLDEN, LTD. PRINTERS, ALDERSHOT.
(69,017). Wt. 7931—443. 40,000 Pads. 4/13. W.

"C" Form (Original). Army Form C. 2123.
MESSAGES AND SIGNALS. No. of Message..............

Prefix S.M. Code M.S. Words 303	Received	Sent, or sent out	Office Stamp
£ s. d.	From..............	At............m.	
Charges to collect	By..............	To..............	
Service Instructions.		By..............	

Handed in at ......T.R.1............ Office ....m. Received ....m.

TO H S   Appendix IV

*Sender's Number	Day of Month	In reply to Number	AAA
AR1/58	22nd		

Intelligence	summary	aaa	Party
of	2 officers	and 3	other
ranks	attempted to	enter	RAVINE
EN 4	last night	aaa	Left
at 6	PM and returned	at 9 PM	
aaa	moved out	to Q10	D 69
aaa	Work was	heard	inside
trench	D 69 and	D 51 aaa	
Wire	consisted of	3 belts	of
very	strong wire	tightly	stretched
which	was cut	only with	
difficulty aaa	First two	belts	
were	cut through	successfully	
and third	belt commenced		
when about	30 feet	from trench	
a very	youthful	voice	shouted
HALTE	several times	aaa	much

FROM
PLACE & TIME

"C" Form (Original).
MESSAGES AND SIGNALS.

Army Form C. 2123.

Prefix	Code	Words	Received From	Sent, or sent out	Office Stamp
	£ s. d.		By	At .... m.	
Charges to collect				To	
Service Instructions.				By	

Handed in at ......T.R.......... Office .... m. Received .... m.

TO: H Q Appendix II

*Sender's Number	Day of Month	In reply to Number	AAA
AR 7			

Patrols have nothing to report aaa Intelligence aaa usual transport aaa to be underground tapping could be heard in officers dugout in rear of trench 52 at 11 AM aaa Work done aaa Rebuilding parapet and parados draining bay aaa and some prepared aaa assault about nil aaa smoke helmets coils aaa R E stores required aaa 2000 sandbags 110 sheets C I aaa 50 6ft stakes aaa trench ladders aaa 4 bags nails aaa 30 rolls expanded metal aaa 30 rolls felt aaa 10 bundles iron stakes short

FROM

PLACE & TIME

* This line should be erased if not required.

"C" Form (Original). Army Form C. 2123.
MESSAGES AND SIGNALS. No. of Message ....

Prefix...... Code...... Words......	Received.	Sent, or sent out	Office Stamp.
£ s. d.	From	At .... m.	
Charges to collect	By	To	
Service Instructions.		By	

Handed in at .... Office .... m. Received .... m.

TO

| *Sender's Number | Day of Month | In reply to Number | AAA |

line is held in normal strength
but sentries are not very
alert or are accustomed to much
work being done in front of them
aaa The rocket referred to was
white and has not previously
been used aaa Effect very good
aaa Great height attained and
very long range aaa During
night German wire heard repairing
cut wire and were fired on by
machine gun aaa further
reference to M 258 at D 69 is
new and was put up after our
bombardment of 25th left aaa
Though very tough it can be

FROM
PLACE & TIME

* This line should be erased if not required.
Wt. 9771/4004. 75,000 Pads. 10/15. McC. & Co., Ltd., London. Forms/C.2123.

"C" Form (Duplicate).
MESSAGES AND SIGNALS.

Army Form C. 2123.

No. of Message ....

	Charges to Pay.	Office Stamp.
	£ s. d.	
Service Instructions.		

Handed in at.................... Office......... m. Received .... m.

TO

Sender's Number	Day of Month	In reply to Number	**AAA**

confusion followed and rapid fire was opened aaa a very fine rocket was sent up which illuminated whole area splendidly and fire became general aaa Patrol threw 2 bombs towards trench and returned without loss soon afterwards aaa Patrol state Germans have a gas or oil engine at work near O.71 and sounds of a trolly or vehicle on line were heard in rear aaa They positively state the following ENGLISH words were used by enemy RAPID FIRE and CEASE FIRE aaa From all appearances the

FROM

PLACE & TIME

"C" Form (Duplicate). — Army Form C. 2123.
MESSAGES AND SIGNALS.

| Service Instructions. | Charges to Pay. £ s. d. | Office Stamp. |

Handed in at................... Office........... m. Received........... m.

TO

| Sender's Number | Day of Month | In reply to Number | A A A |

cut with wire cutters and
In addition to patrol of
five a covering party of 8
men were sent out to
render assistance if needed

FROM: A H Q
PLACE & TIME

Wt. 9771/4001. 75,000 Pads. 10/15. McC. & Co., Ltd., London. Forms/C.2123.

"C" Form (Duplicate).
MESSAGES AND SIGNALS.

Army Form C. 2123.
No. of Message ....

	Charges to Pay.	Office Stamp.
Service Instructions. TR	£ s. d.	

Handed in at .... Office .... m. Received 2.8 P m.

TO: H₂ dose / Appendix Ⅳ   11TH BDE

Sender's Number	Day of Month	In reply to Number	AAA
	23rd		

Tunnelling coy have taken no action as yet beyond listening aaa Capt Towers remained here until 1.30 am and reported he heard nothing aaa Counter work suspended by his directions aaa Capt Edwards reported hostile work going on this morning but in a new direction aaa An Officer of tunnelling coy was here for a short time this morning and reported nothing could be

FROM
PLACE & TIME

Wt. 9771/4094. 75,000 Pads. 10/15. McC. & Co., Ltd., London. Forms/C.2123.

"C" Form (Original).
MESSAGES AND SIGNALS.

Army Form C. 2123.

Prefix AM Code D Words 48

Charges to collect

Service Instructions.

Handed in at T.R.1 Office ... m. Received ... m.

TO: H 8 Appendix II

*Sender's Number	Day of Month	In reply to Number	AAA
AR1/91	29th		

Patrols	last	night	to P 10 D 66
aaa	2	Officers 3	men aaa
Reports	enemy	have	sniping post
150 yards	from	our	lines aaa
Flashes	from	this	point have
been	previously noted	aaa	they
surprised 2	men	at	the
post	aaa	Enemy	retired blew
a	small	whistle and	sent
up a	small	flare	aaa
they	were	chased	up to
a	gap	in	wire where
they	sent	up	another flare
and	fire	was	opened from
German	lines	aaa	Our patrol
penetrated gap	and	retaliated with

FROM

PLACE & TIME

4th Div.
11th Inf.Bde.

WAR DIARY

2ND BATTN. THE ROYAL IRISH REGT.

DECEMBER

1 9 1 5.

(Joined 11th Inf.Bde. 26.7.15 from 12th Inf. Bde.)

Army Form C. 2118.

WAR DIARY
or
INTELLIGENCE SUMMARY.

(Erase heading not required.)

December 1915   2nd Battⁿ The Royal Irish Regt.

Instructions regarding War Diaries and Intelligence
Summaries are contained in F. S. Regs., Part II.
and the Staff Manual respectively. Title pages
will be prepared in manuscript.

Place	Date	Hour	Summary of Events and Information	Remarks and references to Appendices
ENGLEBELMER	Dec 1915		Two companies in trenches; two companies in billets. ENGLEBELMER relieving each other as in November.	
			Following Service Battalions attached during the month for instruction in trench warfare.	
			22nd Bn Manchester Regt - Nov 27 - Dec 4	
			18th Bn Manchester " Dec 7 - " 14	
			17th Bn Liverpool Regt - " 17 - " 25	
			Headquarters Staff 89th Infy Brigade.	
	1-3		Enemy machine guns very active at night's. Sniping on front.	
	4		Patrol of Manchester Regt (attached) encountered a patrol of the enemy & attacked same with bombs & withdrawing without loss.	
	6		2nd Lieut J. Pollock, 3rd Bn Royal Irish Fusiliers, joined the Battⁿ	
	7		2nd Lieut P.L. Blake, rejoined the Battⁿ	
	12		Enemy machine guns again active.	
	13-17		Weather very bad, ceaseless rain. All quiet.	

WAR DIARY or INTELLIGENCE SUMMARY

Army Form C. 2118.

December 1915

2nd Batt: The Royal Irish Regt

Place	Date	Hour	Summary of Events and Information	Remarks and references to Appendices
Continued.	18.		Enemy's trenches badly affected by weather. Seen baling & draining constantly.	
	20.		Patrol under Lieut Power encountered large enemy working party, which was dispersed by our fire & hurriedly retired into German trenches.	
	25.		At about 6.30 p.m., patrol under Lieuts Forde & Grant with 16 men endeavoured to enter German line at point Q10 D 67. They found the first line of enemy wire cut by our artillery. Lieut Forde & 6 men entered gap, remainder forming covering party carrying bombs. About 8.15 pm an alarm was given in German lines and fire was opened. Our party remained still for some time but as enemy appeared to be reinforcing decided to bomb their trenches then about 20 yds distant. Enemy returned fire with very heavy trench type grenade. As action became general and our patrol appeared to be in difficulty, an artillery bombardment on German second line trenches and communication trenches was asked for & complied with. About the same time Germans sent out bombing party from their trenches which	

Army Form C. 2118.

WAR DIARY
INTELLIGENCE SUMMARY.
2nd Batt~ The Royal 2nd Reg^t

December 1915

(Erase heading not required.)

Place	Date	Hour	Summary of Events and Information	Remarks and references to Appendices
Continued			retired on being bombed & fired on by us. Our patrols drew off without loss & regained lines at about 10 p.m. Patrols reported enemy very alert & active in their trenches at intervals of about 25 yards. Wire appeared very strongly held. See Appendix I. Wire of congratulation from G.O.C. 11th Brigade	W.
	Dec 7		2nd Lieut. C.H. Turner joined the Batt~	
	8		Captain Buss joined the Batt~	
			N.B. Casualties for month of December 1915: 2 O.R. killed in action	
			5 O.R. wounded in action	

"C" Form (Original).   Army Form C. 2123 A.

MESSAGES AND SIGNALS.

| Prefix 2M | Code BCH | Words 41 | Received From 2K By JJones Cpl | Sent, or sent out At ... m To ... By ... | Office Stamp. |

Charges to collect

Service Instructions 2K

Handed in at the .... Office, at .... m. Received here at 2.205 m.

TO   I.

Sender's Number	Day of Month	In reply to Number	AAA
R	26	R1/2	

Please congratulate LT FORSTER and GRANT also PTE WRIGHT DEELING and JENKINS and the patrol for their gallant work of last night aaa I have forwarded your report to Division

FROM: BRIGADIER
PLACE:
TIME: 2 pm

11th Brigade.
4th Division.

2nd BATTALION

ROYAL IRISH REGIMENT

JANUARY 1 9 1 6

Army Form C. 2118.

WAR DIARY
or
INTELLIGENCE SUMMARY 2nd Batt. The Royal Irish Regt.

(Erase heading not required.)

Instructions regarding War Diaries and Intelligence Summaries are contained in F. S. Regs., Part II. and the Staff Manual respectively. Title pages will be prepared in manuscript.

Place	Date	Hour	Summary of Events and Information	Remarks and references to Appendices
ENGLEBELMER	January 1916		Two companies in trenches, two companies in billets (ENGLEBELMER) as in Base Diary.	
	1-4		Very quiet.	
	5		Attempted enemy attack on trenches held by E. LANCS on our right, which was repulsed. Considerable rifle & machine gun activity on our front. Appendix I attached.	
	6-7		Very quiet.	
	8		Enemy artillery & machine gun activity. Appendix II attached.	
	9-10		Very quiet.	
	11		Two special patrols were sent out with the object of cutting the enemy's wire & successfully bombing a section of his trenches. The right patrol was unable and the 2nd left patrol under 2nd Lt. Forster. These patrols were successful in cutting a considerable portion of the enemy's wire but eventually came on some wire of a very heavy type which it was impossible to cut; so the patrol returned. The operation was supported by batteries 134 & 136 R.F.A & battery 139 R.G.A, but fire was not opened.	
	12		Appendix III attached re aeroplane activity.	

2353 Wt. W2511/1454 700,000 5/15 D. D. & L.   A.D.S.S./Forms/C. 2118.

Army Form C. 2118.

WAR DIARY (Cont.)
or
INTELLIGENCE SUMMARY. 2nd Bn. The Royal Irish Regt.

(Erase heading not required.)

Instructions regarding War Diaries and Intelligence Summaries are contained in F.S. Regs., Part II. and the Staff Manual respectively. Title pages will be prepared in manuscript.

Place	Date	Hour	Summary of Events and Information	Remarks and references to Appendices
	January 1916.			
	13		Quiet	
	14		Enemy bombarded our trenches with trench mortars. No damage done.	
	15		Quiet.	
	16		Appendix IV attached	
	17		Nothing of interest to report.	
	18		Appendix V attached re bombardment of our trenches.	
	19–26		Quiet. Enemy machine guns active.	
	28		Enemy reported to be using gas against 48 Division on our left. No effects were felt on our front.	
	30		Billets in ENGHELBELMER shelled. No damage resulted.	
			Casualties to during January. O.R. 1 Killed 3 wounded	

11th Brigade.
4th Division.

2nd BATTALION

ROYAL IRISH REGIMENT

FEBRUARY 1 9 1 6

Operation Orders attached:

WAR DIARY 2nd Battn. the Royal Irish Rgt Army Form C. 2118.
or
INTELLIGENCE SUMMARY

(Erase heading not required.)

Vol 1v2 + 13

Hour, Date, Place	Summary of Events and Information	Remarks and references to Appendices
ENGLEBELMER 1916 Feby 5-	Trenches. Baptism on relief as in January	
6	At about 8 pm the Battalion was relieved in the trenches by the 11th Bn. the Royal Irish Rifles	
7	During our occupation of this line opposite the RAVIN EN-Y and EAST of AUCHONVILLERS namely from Aug 1r to Feb 16 there were 49 casualties in all; 2 killed & 47 wounded	
	At 12.30 pm the Battn. marched out of ENGLEBELMER for VARENNES which village was reached about 4 pm that afternoon.	
8	At 9 am the march was continued to TERRAMESNIL via ARQUIEVES – BEAUQUESNE	
9	Village of TERRAMESNIL deemed to be very dirty and insanitary	
10	Owing to the insanitary conditions of TERRAMESNIL the Battalion was moved to BERNVAL.	
11-17	Rest billets and training at BERNVAL.	
18	The Battn. marched in Brigade to S.S. ST-LEGER, Royal Irish leading	
19-24	Rest and training at S.S. ST-LEGER	
25-	Sudden move to GEZAINCOURT. The march from S.S. ST LEGER to GEZAINCOURT was carried out in a heavy fog and snow	
26-29	GEZAINCOURT – ACHEUX training for Brigade Sports.	

"C" Form (Original)
Army Form C. 2123
MESSAGES AND SIGNALS.
No. of Message ....

Prefix .... Code .1.30. Words ....
Received From TR1 By Dates
Sent, or sent out At ...... m. To ...... By ......
Office Stamp

Charges to collect
Service Instructions.

Handed in at .... TR1 .... Office ...... m. Received 1.47½ m.

TO   H. Q. I.

*Sender's Number	Day of Month	In reply to Number	AAA
OR 16	3rd		

Intelligence aaa Enemy party of 10 observed working in or near dos in RAVINE of Sam this moment aaa our artillery obtained a direct hit and two stretcher bearers were afterwards seen aaa They were apparently wearing steel round hats and dark coloured jackets aaa at 10.30 am a fire broke out in enemy front trenches immediately in front 1.30 trenches probably without a aaa Smoke helmets correct aaa Casualties aaa a Coy 8171

FROM
PLACE & TIME

Copy No. 1.

OPERATION ORDER NO.1.
BY,
LIEUT. COLONEL W.J. DUGAN, D.S.O.,
COMMANDING 2ND. BN. THE ROYAL IRISH REGIMENT.

Reference Map FRANCE 1:40,000　　　　The Field
　　　Sheet 57 D.　　　　　　　　　　　6/2/16.

1.
1. The Battalion will move to Rest Billets at TERRAMESNIL (H.19).
2. The first march will be VARENNES (P.25) where the Battalion will be billeted for the night 7th./8th. February.
3. Starting Point- Road junction P.34.D5.9.
4. Companies and other units, in the order shewn in attached March Table, will move to the Starting Point independently passing No.2. examining guard ENGLEBELMER on the 7th. inst., at the times stated below:-

Signallers and H.Q Orderlies .... 1.50.p.m.
"A" Company .... 1.55. "
"B"   "   .... 2.0. "
"C"   "   .... 2.5. "
"D"   "   .... 2.10. "
Regtl. Police, Prisoners,　)
Pioneers, Machine Gunners,)............ 2.15. "
and Limbers.   )
Medical Officer and Cart,)
Pack animals, Spare horses)............ 2.20. "
and Transport.   )

On arrival at the Starting Point the above units will fall out clear of the road and await orders to march off in column of route.

　　　　　　　　T. A. LOWE, CAPTAIN & ADJUTANT,
　　　2ND. BATTALION THE ROYAL IRISH REGIMENT.

Hour of Issue.

Copy No. 1.　　　War Diary.
 "   No. 2.　　　O.C. "A" Coy.
 "   No. 3.　　　 "   "B" "
 "   No. 4.　　　 "   "C" "
 "   No. 5.　　　 "   "D" "
 "   No. 6.　　　T.O.
 "   No. 7.　　　M.G.O.
 "   No. 8.　　　Med. Offr.

Copy No. 1.

OPERATION ORDER No. 2.

By

LIEUT.COLONEL W.J. CURRAN, D.S.O.
COMMANDING 2ND BATTALION THE ROYAL IRISH REGIMENT.

Reference Map, France 57 D.   THE FIELD.
            1:40,000.   7. 2. 16.

===========================

1. The Battalion will march to FIENVILLERS tomorrow

2. ROUTE: HEILLYBRAND - RAINNEVILLE - BEAUVAL(?)

3. STARTING POINT - Road junction P.29 a-3-3.

4. The head of the Battalion ("B" Company leading)
   in column of route in the order of march issued with
   Operation Order No 1. will be at the Starting Point
   at 8.0a.m. ready to move off.

5. REVEILLE at 5.5.a.m.

6. All company will be issued at the Bivouacs.

7. Breakfasts will be at 7.30 a.m.

                                Lieut. Captain & Adjutant.
                                2nd Bn. The Royal Irish Regt.

   Copy No. 1. O.C.
   "   No. 2. "B" Company.
   "   No. 3. "C"   "
   "   No. 4. "D"   "
   "   No. 5. "A"   "
   "   No. 6. Medical Officer.
   "   No. 7. War Diary Battalion.

Copy..........1..........

OPERATION ORDER No. 3.
By.
LIEUT.COLONEL. W.J.DUGAN. D.S.O.
COMMANDING 2ND.BN. THE ROYAL IRISH REGIMENT.
Reference Map France.   The Field. 9/3/16
    :40,000
    Sheet 57. D.

==

1. The Battalion will march to BEAUVAL tomorrow.

2. STARTING POINT - Road Junction G.24.D.8.9.

3. The head of the Battalion in the Order of March as shown in March table issued with Operation Order No.1. ("C" Company leading) will be at S.P. ready to move off in column of route at 2.p.m.

4. Dinners 12 noon

5. Waggons to be loaded up at 11.30.

6. All surplus kits including blankets and skin coats to be at Q.Mr stores at 11.a.m. The company on duty will furnish a guard (1 N.C.O. and 3 men at Q.M. stores.

                    T.A.LOWE. CAPTAIN & ADJUTANT,
              2ND.BATTALION THE ROYAL IRISH REGIMENT.
Hour of issue 10.p.m.

Copy No.1.   War Diary.
Copy No.2.   O.C. "A" Coy.
  "   No.3.   "   "B" "
  "   No.4.   "   "C" "
  "   No.5.   "   "D" "
  "   No.6.   "   T.O.
  "   No.7.   M.G.O.
  "   No.8.   Med. Offr.

Copy No. 1

OPERATION ORDER No. 4.
By,
LIEUT:COLONEL W.J. DUGAN. D.S.O.
COMMANDING 2ND.BN. THE ROYAL IRISH REGIMENT.

Reference Sheet 11 Lens.　　　　　　　　The Field
　　　1/100,000　　　　　　　　　　February. 17th.1916.

------

1. The Battalion will march in Brigade tomorrow to SUS - St - LEGER. (F4) Route - DOULLENS - LUCHEUX - TUILIE - Cross Roads 1/4 mile S of Q in SUS - St LEGER.

2. The Battalion will be formed up in column of Route ready to move off ("A" Coy leading) in the open space opposite the Church at 8.45.a.m.
Regimental Transport will be formed up ready to move off in rear of the Battalion according to special instructions issued to the Transport Officer.

3. Sick will be seen at 7.a.m.

4. Breakfasts at 7.30.a.m.

5. All baggage to be loaded up by 7.30.a.m.

6. Baggage Guard. 1 N.C.O. & 10 men detailed by the Quarter Master.

7. A special haversack ration for use on the march only, will be issued at Q.M. Stores at 7.50.a.m.

8. The Coy on duty will detail a rear party of 1 Officer & 20 men to tidy up billets. This Officer will report to a Staff Officer of the Brigade when all billets are clean. He will then follow the Battalion.

9. A representative of each Coy & Transport will attend at the Orderly Room at 7.30.a.m to compare watches.

　　　　T. A. LOWE, CAPTAIN & ADJUTANT,
　　　2ND. BATTALION THE ROYAL IRISH REGIMENT.

Hour of issue. 6.30 p.m.
Copy No.1.　　　War Diary.
　"　No.2.　　　O.C. "A" Coy.
　"　No.3.　　　"　"B"　"
　"　No.4.　　　"　"C"　"
　"　No.5.　　　"　"D"　"
　"　No.6.　　　T.O.
　"　No.7.　　　R.C.O.
　"　No.8.　　　Med. Offr.

COPY No 1.

2nd Bn The Royal Irish Regt. Order No 5.
Reference - France Sheet 51c.

1. The Battalion will move to GROUCHES (S.25 and 26.) to-day.
2. Route — TUILERIE in O.31 — LUCHEUX.
3. Starting Point — TUILERIE O.31-a-2-0.
4. The Battalion will be formed up in column of route ("C" Coy leading) at the Starting Point at 1-15 p.m.
5. All baggage to be dumped at Regimental Bath opposite the Brigade Institute by 9 a.m.
6. <u>Dinners</u> — at 12 noon
7. <u>Rear Party</u> — The Coy. on duty will detail a rear party of 1 Officer and 15 men to clean up Billets after the departure of the Battalion. This party will rejoin the Battalion at GROUCHES
8. <u>Dress</u> — Marching Order — Troops will carry their fur coats rolled on the top of the Pack
Hour of issue – 8 a.m.
Copy No. 1 – War Diary
 "   " 2 – O.C. "A"
 "   " 3 – O.C. "B"
 "   " 4 – O.C. "C"
 "   " 5 – O.C. "D"
 "   " 6 – T.
 "   " 7 – M.G.O
 "   " 8 – M.O

(Sd) T.A. LOWE, CAPTAIN

ADJUTANT 2/ THE ROYAL IRISH REGT.

11th Brigade.

4th Division.

2nd BATTALION

ROYAL IRISH REGIMENT

MARCH 1 9 1 6

WAR DIARY
or
INTELLIGENCE SUMMARY
(Erase heading not required.)

Army Form C. 2118.

Instructions regarding War Diaries and Intelligence Summaries are contained in F. S. Regs., Part II. and the Staff Manual respectively. Title pages will be prepared in manuscript.

Hour, Date, Place	Summary of Events and Information	Remarks and references to Appendices
GROUCHES Mar 1/6	Revl billets. Weather very severe, food scarce.	
6	The Battalion marched from Grouches to Brewilers	
6/16 BREWILERS	Coy & Battn. Training carried out	
"	– do – St Patricks day. Sports were held and a special dinner prepared for the men	
18	The Battalion marched to Souastre	
19	From Souastre to close support, two companies in Fonquevillers, two companies in Monchiennes.	
20/23	Close support to the 11th Suff. Bde.	
24	The Battalion moved into the line relieving the 1/5 Lancs Fus	
25-	Weather in trenches very bad. No shelters of any kind.	
26	Still severe. One man killed by a rifle grenade.	
29	Relief march to rest billets in Pommier	
30	POMMIER	

R.P. Guppy
Lieut-Colonel
Comdg 2nd Bn The Royal Irish

Copy No 1

2nd BATTALION THE ROYAL IRISH REGIMENT.
ORDER NO. 5.

Reference FRANCE.   Sheet 51c   5/3/16.

1. The Battalion will march to BREVILLERS tomorrow.
   Route: LUCHEUX - X roads T.8.b. - BREVILLERS.

2. STARTING POINT.- Last house N.E. end of GROUCHES.

3. The Battalion will be formed up in column of route
   ("B" Coy. leading) with the head at the Starting
   Point at 10.30.a.m.

4. Fur coats will be carried, rolled on the top of the
   pack.

5. Baggage will be loaded up by 9.30.a.m.

6. REAR PARTY. The Coy. on duty will detail one Officer
   and 15 men to remain behind and see billets cleaned
   up. This party will rejoin the Battn. at BREVILLERS.

7. BREAKFASTS.----- 8.a.m.
   SICK PARADE.---- 8.30.a.m.
   C.O's. ORDERS.--- 9.a.m.

        (Sd.) T.A.LOWE, CAPTAIN & ADJUTANT,
                2nd. Battalion The Royal Irish Regiment.

Hour Of Issue. 6.40 pm
Copy No. 1 .... War Diary.
  ,,   2 .... O.C. "B" Coy.
  ,,   3 .... O.C. "C" ,,
  ,,   4 .... O.C. "D" ,,
  ,,   5 .... T.O.
  ,,   6 .... M.G.O.
  ,,   7 .... M.O.

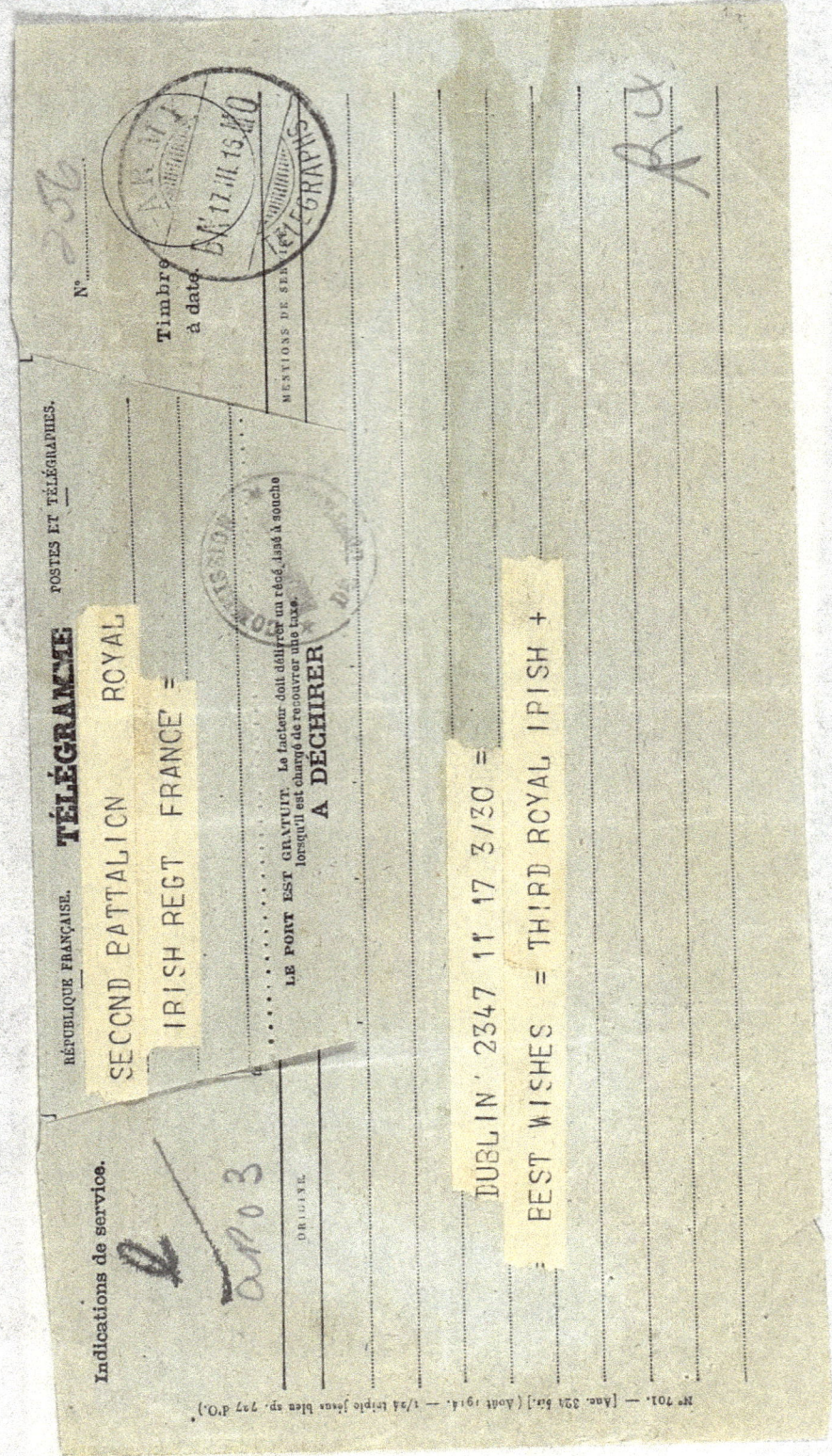

Signification des principales indications éventuelles pouvant figurer en tête de l'adresse.

D..... = Urgent.
AR.... = Remettre contre reçu.
PC.... = Accusé de réception.
RP.... = Réponse payée.
TC.... = Télégramme collationné.
MP.... = Remettre en mains propres.

XPx.... = Exprès payé.
NUIT... = Remettre même pendant la nuit.
JOUR... = Remettre seulement pendant le jour.
OUVERT = Remettre ouvert.

Dans les télégrammes imprimés en caractères romains par l'appareil télégraphique, le premier nombre qui figure après le nom du lieu d'origine est un numéro d'ordre, le second indique le nombre de mots taxés, les autres désignent la date et l'heure du dépôt. Dans le service intérieur et dans les relations avec certains pays étrangers, l'heure de dépôt est indiquée au moyen des chiffres de 0 à 24.

L'État n'est soumis à aucune responsabilité à raison du service de la correspondance privée par la voie télégraphique. (Loi du 29 novembre 1850, art. 6.)

Indications de service.

N° ...256...

Timbre à date

DUBLIN 2347 11 17 3/30 =
BEST WISHES = THIRD ROYAL IPISH +

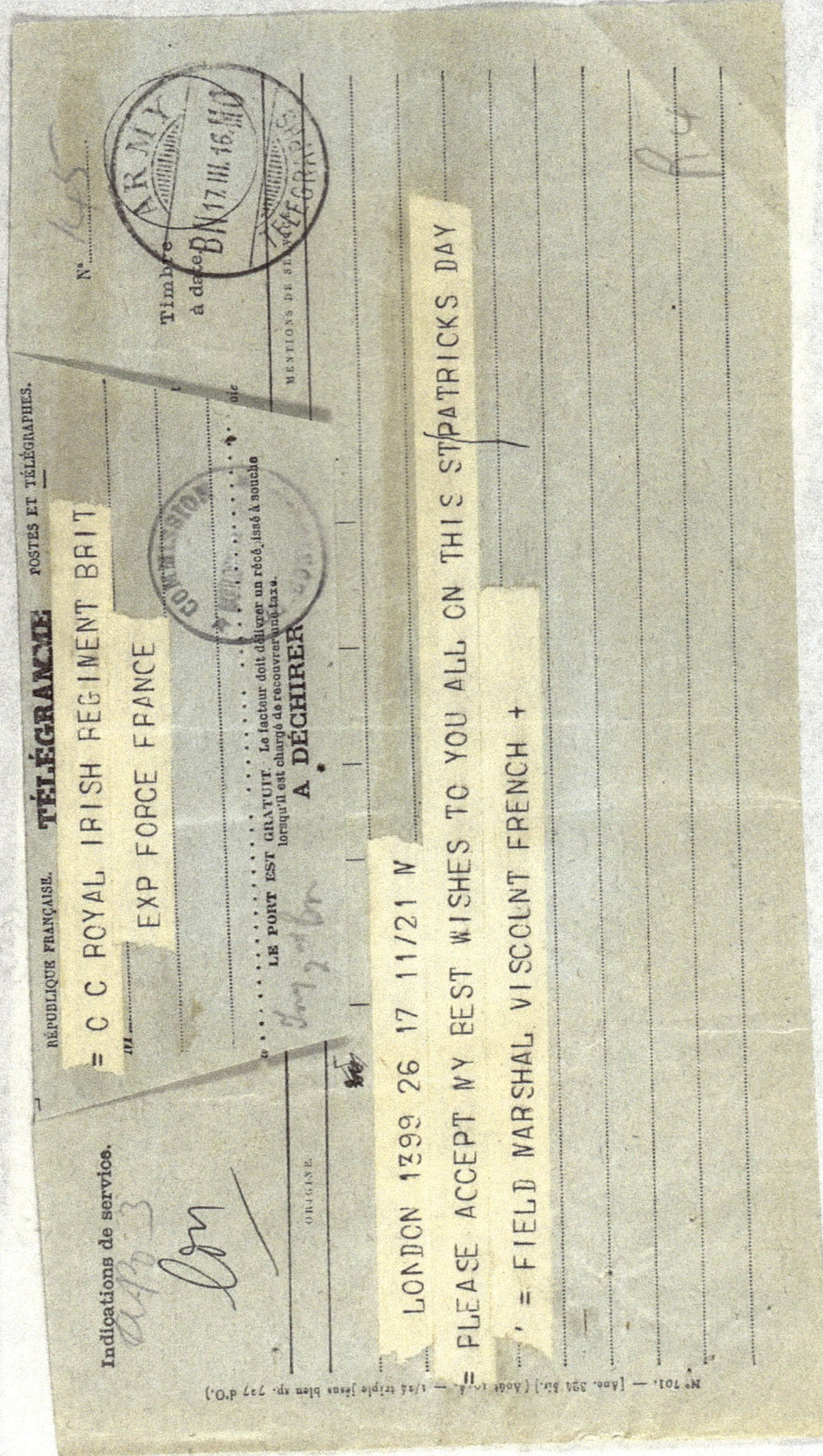

LONDON 1399 26 17 11/21 M

PLEASE ACCEPT MY BEST WISHES TO YOU ALL ON THIS ST PATRICKS DAY

= FIELD MARSHAL, VISCOUNT FRENCH +

"C" Form (Duplicate).
MESSAGES AND SIGNALS.

Army Form C. 2123.
No. of Message 65

| | Charges to Pay. £ s. d. | Office Stamp. |

Service Instructions.

Handed in at .... Office .... m. Received .... m.

TO .... Roy. Irish ....

| Sender's Number | Day of Month | In reply to Number | **A A A** |

Best wishes to all Ranks Royal Irish for St Patrick's Day

FROM
PLACE & TIME Gen'l Munro

2nd Battalion The Royal Irish Regiment. Order No. 6.

Reference Map. Lens 11.   18th March 1916.

1. The Battalion will march to SOUASTRE today.
   Route: LUCHEUX--POMMERA--PAS--HENU.

2. Starting Point. Crucifix S.E. end of Village.

3. Companies will be formed up at the Starting Point ready to move off at 1.45p.m. ("A" Company leading)

4. On reaching HENU Companies will go forward to SOUASTRE at intervals of 5 minutes between Coys.

      (Sd.) T.A.LOWE, CAPTAIN & ADJUTANT,
        2nd Battalion The Royal Irish Regt.

Copy No.1. War Diary.
 ,, No.2. O.C. "A" Coy.
 ,, No.3. O.C. "B" ,,
 ,, No.4. O.C. "D" ,,
 ,, No.5. M.O.
 ,, No.6. M.G.C.
 ,, No.7. T.O.

2nd Battalion The Royal Irish Regiment.
Operation Order no. 7.

Reference map Lens 11.   19.3.16.

1. The Battalion will relieve the 6th. Bn. Bedfordshire Regt. this evening.

2. (a) The leading platoon of the Right Detachment (A & B Companies) will arrive at western barrier FONQUEVILLERS on FONQUEVILLERS-SOUASTRE Road at 6.45 p.m.

(b) The leading platoon of the two companies for left detachment HANNESCAMPS (C & D Coys) will arrive at eastern barrier of BIENVILLERS on BIENVILLERS-HANNESCAMPS Road at 6.45 p.m.

3. Guides. 1 Officer per Coy. 1 man per platoon and two Lewis gunners 6/Bedfordshire Regt. will meet the platoons and guns of the Battn. on arrival at the barriers mentioned in 2 (a) and 2 (b) respectively.

4. The Regimental Transport may enter FONQUEVILLERS at 8.15 p.m. and HANNESCAMPS at 8.45 p.m.

5. All trench stores, ammunition, grenades, maps &c. will be taken over from 6th. Bn. Bedfordshire Regt in daylight. Lieut. Tod and Lieut. Hegarty will proceed to HANNESCAMPS and FONQUEVILLERS respectively at 2 p.m. for this purpose. They should make lists in duplicate of all stores taken over and forward one copy to the Orderly Room by 12 noon tomorrow. The other copy will be handed to the O.C. detachment who will cause copies

to be made out for handing over on relief. These officers will move via BIENVILLERS.

6. The Lewis Machine Gun officer will detail three guns to accompany each detachment. Numbers of each L.G. detachment should be notified to the Q.M. who will make necessary arrangements for rations.

7. The Signalling Sergeant will detail 2 parties of 3 signallers to leave SOUASTRE at 3 p.m. and proceed to FONQUEVILLERS and HANNESCAMPS respectively to take over the stations there. They should arrive by 4 p.m. with instruments etc. and report to O.C. detachment 6th Bedfordshire Regt. in these places. They will move via BIENVILLERS.

8. Reports.
O.C. detachments will report to Bn. Hqrs. when relief is completed.

SECRET.   Copy No. 1

2nd Bn. The Royal Irish Regiment
Order No 8.

Reference French Map Sheet 57d
  N.E. pts 1 & 2.   23.3.'16.

1. The Battn. will relieve the 1/East Lancashire Regt in the trenches tomorrow evening.
   Companies will hold the line from right to left in the following order:-

   A. B. C.   In support D. Coy.

2. As soon as it is dark A Coy will move into the line by the right, and relieve the Right Coy 1/E Lancs Regt. C Coy will move into the line via CHISWICK AV. and relieve the Left Company 1/E Lancs. B Coy will remain at FONQUEVILLERS until relieved by a company of the Som L.I. when it will move into the line, and take up its position as CENTRE Coy of the line. D Coy. will remain at HANNESCAMPS until relieved by a Coy. of the Som L.I. when it will move into the line in Support at SNIPERS. SQ.

   Lewis Guns will be relieved under arrangements to be made by the Lewis M.G. Officer.

3. In addition to his ordinary equipment each man will carry into the line, one blanket, his oilsheet & waterproof cape. The remaining blankets & Officers kits will be rolled & stacked in a convenient place in FONQUEVILLERS and HANNESCAMPS, under a loading party of 1 N.C.O. and 5 men to be detailed by B & D Coy. respectively. These will be taken back to the transport lines under arrangements to be made by the Transport Officer.

4. Battn. H.Qrs. will close at BIENVILLERS at 7 p.m. and reopen at FONQUEVILLERS at

the same hour. Special attention is
directed, to the instructions accompanying
this order.

5. Companies will report by wire to Battn.
H.Qrs. as soon as they have taken over
the line.

(Sd) I.H. Lowe Captain & adjutant
2/The Royal Irish Regt.

Copy No 1   War Diary
      2   O.C.   A
      3   O.C.   B
      4   O.C.   C
      5   O.C.   D
      6   M.O.
      7   T.O.
      8   Lewis M G O.

Issued with Order No. 8.   Dated 23/3/16.

Special Instructions re the taking over of
the Line

(1) It is possible that the Germans have received information of a relief having taken place & may make some attempt to identify the troops opposed to them in this Sector. Special precautions are therefore called for from all ranks to prevent hostile parties approaching our lines & taking prisoners, as well as for dealing with any patrol which may have effected an entry.

(2) The Battn. Grenadier Officer will in consultation with the Coy Commanders make arrangements:-
(a) for a supply of bombs to be held ready for instant use in the front trenches.
(b) for Grenadiers to be posted at suitable points in the front line to deal with such attempts on the part of the enemy as those mentioned in para 1.

3. For the first night in order to give all ranks an opportunity of becoming acquainted with the ground, trench line etc, no patrols will be sent out without special orders from Bn H.Qrs. but listening posts will be placed at frequent intervals inside our own wire.

Special care is to be taken that Sentries on the flanks of the Battn. are in touch with those of other Units. If necessary flying sentries should be posted to ensure this.

4. As our line is somewhat overlooked by the enemy all ranks must be careful to avoid exposing themselves by day.

5. As soon as Companies take up their positions in the trenches, 2 Orderlies per Coy. will be specially detailed to make themselves acquainted with the shortest way to Bn. H.Qrs. & to the H.Qrs. of the Support Company.

All Officers of the Support Company will personally reconnoitre the best way to reinforce any part of the front line.

6. Where large shelters exist a sentry will be posted by night in the entrance to warn the occupants in the case of a gas attack or any other alarm.

7. Men sleeping in shelters will have their rifles beside them and bayonets fixed. Officers on duty will invariably be armed and equipped & by night will carry a Very pistol & six cartridges.

8. The Routine laid down in Battn & 3/Army Trench Orders will be strictly adhered to. The following paras in 3rd Army Trench Orders will be specially noted:-

    1 (h)   12 (i)   27 (b)
    3 (a)   12 (j)   27 (c)
    5 (g)   12 (k)   27 (e)
            15 (a)

9. The hours of "Stand to" will be notified later.

10. The Battn. Grenadier will carry out the weekly test of grenades on Sat morning next and will report the result to Battn H.Q. when he has done so.

11. Company Commanders will ascertain from the Commanders of Companies they are relieving whether any material has to be carried to their sector of the trench. If so they should arrange to carry it during the process of relief; it should be noted that the wire in front of our line is very bad.

12. In order to prevent delay & the danger of men losing their way the ration parties of "A" & "C" Coys will not be detailed on the first night until after these 2 coys have arrived in the line. The rations for "B" & "D" Coys will probably have arrived before the Coys. move off, if not, the same procedure will be adopted.

13. Anti frost bite grease will be issued tonight & the usual feet rubbing procedure will be carried out tomorrow prior to going into the line.

(Sd) J A Lowe, Captain & Adjutant
2/The Royal Irish Regiment

2nd Battalion The Royal Irish Regt.   Copy No 1
Order no. 9
Reference trench map. FONQUEVILLERS   26.3.16.

1. A new trench and entanglement will be constructed tomorrow night from FORT A (NORTH FORTIN) to Junction of trenches 56 and 57. Lanes in the existing wire just NORTH of NORTH FORTIN and in front of trench 56/57 have already been cut.

2. The entrenching will be carried out by:-
   (a) First relief - 1/5 O.M.L.I. Strength 2 Officers 110 men.
   (b) Second relief - 1/E. LANCS.   "   2 " 110 "

Each relief will detail 100 men for digging and 10 men for filling sandbags. The first relief will carry 110 shovels and 15 picks. 15 Sappers from the Durham R.E. will be attached to each relief and will lay sandbags. The first relief (1/5 O.M.L.I.) will parade at 6.30 p.m. at Trench Headquarters FONQUEVILLERS will draw tools and proceed under R.E. guide via ROBERTS AVE LA BRAYELLE Rd to TRENCH 56. It will cross the parapet at the junction of trenches 56 & 57 where Lt Triggs will point out tasks.

This relief will face approximately East, place arms and equipment in REAR of trench, and throw earth to the FRONT to form parapet. When tasks are completed the first relief will cease work, place shovels at LEFT of task, put on equipment etc and file out via trench 56 and return via LA BRAYELLE RD to FONQUEVILLERS where it will dismiss. Orders for this relief to cease work will be issued by Lt Triggs R.E.

Second relief (1/E LANCS. REGT.) will march from POMMIER via HANNESCAMPS and then up HANNESCAMPS - LA BRAYELLE RD to front line trenches, follow front line trench to Junction of trenches 56 and 57, reaching this Junction at 9.45 p.m. where 15 Sappers will join the relief. The relief will close up and remain NORTH of Junction until orders are issued for them to move to their tasks. Lt TRIGGS R.E. will detail work for the party.
They will place rifles and equipment on the FRONT of the trench and throw earth to the REAR to form the parados.
When the trench is completed this relief will proceed to FONQUEVILLERS via LA BRAYELLE RD hand over tools at trench Headquarters, draw tea, and return to POMMIER.
The order for this relief to cease work will be given by the R.E. Officer.

3. Wiring party found by "C" Coy 2/R.I
   No.1 party 25 men under Lt MacGrath
   No.2 party 25 "   "   2/Lt Kenny
Special instructions as to form of entanglements have already been issued to these Officers.
Both parties will be adjacent to the gap at JUNCTION trenches 56/57 at dusk (6.45 p.m.)
When covering party, referred to para 4 is in position No 1 party will move through the gap to FORT A, draw materials from dump there, and commence work. No 2 party will work S.E. from the gap and draw materials from dump in trench 56.

4. Covering parties found by "D" Coy 2/R.I
First relief to be in position by 7 p.m on a line which will be pointed out by Major Lyons.
Lieut Usher, and 20 men remaining out until about 10.15 p.m when they will be relieved by a similar party under command of Capt Bell. The second relief will remain in position as a covering party until it receives instructions that the work is completed, when it will and withdraw and rejoin its Company.
A proportion of Grenadiers will form part of these parties.
All movements of each party will be via Gap at Junction trenches 56/57

5. If the enemy opens fire with artillery or machine guns all ranks will at once lie down and remain quiet until the firing has ceased.

2

6. The M.O. will arrange for a forward dressing station in Trench 56. A suitable site will be selected, and placed at his disposal by "D" Coy.

8. Major W.B. LYONS 2/R.I. will supervise work generally and regulate traffic at Gap opposite Trenches 56/57
This Officer will wear a white Brassard.

(Sd) J.A. Lowe, Captain & Adjutant
2/ Royal Irish Regiment

Issued at 8.30 pm

	Copy No 1	War Diary
	2	O.C. "A" Coy 2R.I.
	3	O.C. "B" " "
	4	O.C. "C" " "
	5	O.C. "D" " "
	6	Lewis M.G. O " "
	7	M.O.
	8	11 Inf. Brigade
	9	1/Som. L.I.
	10	1/E. Lancs.
	11	Lt. Triggs R.E.

"A" Form.
MESSAGES AND SIGNALS.
Army Form C. 2121.

Prefix SM	Code 9.15 m	Words 22	Charge	This message is on a/c of:	Recd. at 9.22 p.m.
Office of Origin and Service Instructions. XX		Sent At ...m. To ... By ...		.... Service. (Signature of "Franking Officer.")	Date 27-3-16 From XX By O'Connell

TO — H Q

| Sender's Number. | Day of Month. 27th | In reply to Number. | A A A |

All going well aaa Work delayed owing to nature of ground but going satisfactory

From — A MAJ. LYONS
Place
Time 9.15 PM

"A" Form.
MESSAGES AND SIGNALS.
Army Form C. 2121.
No. of Message ....

| Prefix S.M. Code K.E.A. | Words 11 | Charge | This message is on a/c of: | Recd. at 10.17 Pm |
| Office of Origin and Service Instructions. XX | Sent At ......m To ...... By ...... | | ......Service. (Signature of "Franking Officer.") | Date 27-3-16 From By Connell |

TO | H | Q | | |

| Sender's Number | Day of Month 27th | In reply to Number. | A A A |

All going well

From MAJ LYONS
Place
Time 10.15

"A" Form. Army Form C. 2121.
MESSAGES AND SIGNALS.

| Prefix S7 Code 11 m. | Words 28 | Charge | This message is on a/c of: | Recd. at 10 P m. |
| Office of Origin and Service Instructions. DX | Sent At m. To By | | Service. (Signature of "Franking Officer.") | Date 27-3-16 From DX By O'Connell |

TO — H Q

| Sender's Number. | Day of Month. 27 | In reply to Number. | A A A |

Please arrange to have 40 iron stakes and 10 rolls. barbed wire brought from RE Yard to SNIPERS SQUARE at once

From MAJ LYONS

"A" Form.
Army Form C. 2121.
MESSAGES AND SIGNALS.
No. of Message ....

Prefix S.M. Code L.G.P.m. Words 50 Charge

Office of Origin and Service Instructions.

XX

Sent At .... m. To .... By ....

This message is on a/c of:

.... Service.

(Signature of "Franking Officer.")

Recd. at 11:38 P.m.
Date 27-3-16
From XX
By H. Connell

TO — H Q

Sender's Number.
Day of Month. 27th
In reply to Number.
A A A

The wiring party from B Coy should now come up bringing screw stakes at least 2 per man aaa Stakes are in SNIPERS SQ and at end of LABRAYELLE road aaa Route via LABRAYELLE road to point where trench 57 joins the road thence up 57 aaa Officers should report to me aaa This party will work till dawn

From MAJ LYONS

Place

Time

The above may be forwarded as now corrected. (Z)

.... Censor. Signature of Addresser or person authorised to telegraph in his name.

" This line should be erased if not required.

"A" Form.   Army Form C. 2121.
MESSAGES AND SIGNALS.

Prefix S.17 Code 1 R m. Words 44 Charge | This message is on a/c of: | Recd. at 1.4 A.m.
Date 28-3-16
From XX
By Connell

Office of Origin and Service Instructions. XX

TO — H Q

Sender's Number | Day of Month 28 | In reply to Number | A A A

As far as I can discover there is ~~a gap~~ a gap of 30 yds N.W of FORT A aaa Remainder appears continuous but of course very weak aaa All going well aaa Please hasten party from b. Coy also shovels

From MAJ LYONS
Place
Time 1 AM

"A" Form. Army Form C. 2121.
MESSAGES AND SIGNALS. No. of Message ....

Prefix SM Code IF P. m. Words 27 Charge
Office of Origin and Service Instructions.
XX
Sent
At .... m.
To ....
By ....

This message is on a/s of:
.... Service.
(Signature of "Franking Officer.")

Recd. at 9.39 P. m.
Date 27-3-16
From XX
By O'Connell

TO — H Q

Sender's Number. Day of Month. 27th In reply to Number. A A A

Warn 20 men b Coy under 2 officers if possible to stand by for wiring if required aaa Probably required ~~mid~~ midnight

From MAJ LYONS
Place
Time

Copy No. 1.

2nd. Battalion The Royal Irish Regiment.
Order No. 10.
Reference Trench Map FONQUEVILLERS. $\frac{1}{10000}$ 29-3-16.

1. The Battalion will be relieved in the trenches tomorrow evening by the 1/East Lancs. Regt.

2. Companies will arrange to have guides, 1 N.C.O. per platoon at the following points to take Companies of the 1/East Lancs. Regt. into the line:-
   Right Coy. and Support Coy. at Trench Headquarters FONQUEVILLERS by 7PM.
   Left Coy and Centre Coy at Crucifix HANNESCAMPS (E 16 a 5.7) by 7PM.

3. Lewis Guns and Signallers will be relieved at 4PM.

4. Trench stores etc will be collected cleaned and placed in a central place in each Company line ready for handing over.
   Duplicate lists of these will be prepared, one copy to be receipted by O.C. Coy. of the relieving Battalion and forwarded to the Orderly Room by 10 am. 31st. inst. The other copy will be handed over to the Officer Commanding the relieving company. A detail of work completed and proposed will also be handed over in a similar manner. All trenches latrines etc. will be thoroughly cleaned before handing over.

5. Blankets and waterproof sheets and officers trench kits will be rolled and dumped as under by 6.30pm.
   Hqr. details, Right and Support Coys. under charge of Hq. Guard FONQUEVILLERS.
   Left and Centre under charge of a guard to be found by "C" Coy. at HANNESCAMPS.
   The Regimental Transport Officer will arrange for transport of these to POMMIER.

6. When relieved Companies will proceed independently ~~independently~~ by platoons at 3 minutes interval. to billets in POMMIER via the following routes.

Right and Support Coys.
 FONQUEVILLERS — Rd. junction E.21.b.3.4. — BIENVILLERS — Cross Roads E.2.d.5.4. (BIENVILLERS Church) — POMMIER.

Left and Centre Coys.
 HANNESCAMPS — BIENVILLERS — Cross Roads E.2.d.5.4. (BIENVILLERS Church) — POMMIER

Attention of O.C. Coys. is directed to 3rd. Army Trench Orders paras 24 and 26.

7. Advance parties. Lieuts. Swyny and Nevill, Coy. Quartermaster Sergts. and 1 guide per platoon from each Coy in the line will proceed to POMMIER during tomorrow afternoon to take over billets. These guides will meet their platoons on arrival at POMMIER at the S.E. end of the village.

Lieut. Swyny will make the necessary arrangements for these guides to be ready to meet their platoons at the place indicated.

8. Battalion Headquarters will close at FONQUEVILLERS at 8 p.m. and open at POMMIER at the same hour.

(Sd.) S. A. Lowe, Captain & Adjutant.
 2nd. Battalion, The Royal Irish Regiment.

Hour of issue 4 p.m.

 Copy No 1.   War Diary
      2.   O.C. "A" Coy
      3.   O.C. "B" "
      4.   O.C. "C" "
      5.   O.C. "D" "
      6.   T.O.
      7.   Lieut. Swyny.
      8.   M.O.
      9.   1/E. Lancs. Regt.

11th Brigade.
4th Division.

2nd BATTALION

ROYAL IRISH REGIMENT

APRIL 1 9 1 6

Attached:- Operation Orders.
Situation wires.

WAR DIARY 2nd Batt~ The Royal Irish Regt
Army Form C. 2118.

or

INTELLIGENCE SUMMARY. April 1916.

(Erase heading not required.)

Instructions regarding War Diaries and Intelligence Summaries are contained in F. S. Regs., Part II. and the Staff Manual respectively. Title pages will be prepared in manuscript.

Place	Date	Hour	Summary of Events and Information	Remarks and references to Appendices
	April 1916			
	1-3		Rest billets POMMIER.	
	4		Relief in trenches. Operation Order No 11 attached.	
	5-10		Trenches.	
	11		Battalion in close support. Operation Order No 12 attached.	
	11-16		Close Support.	
	17		Operation Order No 13 attached. Trenches. The special patrol report attached. B & C 11 Brigade congratulated the Battalion on the result of this patrol which returned without casualties having gained valuable information.	
	18		Another special patrol sent out. Order & notes showing progress attached.	
	19-22		Trenches.	
	23		Rest billets POMMIER. Order No 14 attached.	
	24-28		Rest billets POMMIER.	
	29-30		Trenches. See Operation Order No 15 attached	

102.

"C" Form (Duplicate).   Army Form C. 2123.
MESSAGES AND SIGNALS.   No. of Message ....

| Service Instructions. | Charges to Pay. £ s. d. | Office Stamp |

Handed in at................Office..........m. Received...........m.

TO: Right Co, A.1.

Sender's Number	Day of Month	In reply to Number	AAA
D.10	18		

Endeavour to get into touch with Lieut FORSTER who is in vicinity of POPLAR and report result AAA Small patrol should be used for this purpose AAA

FROM: HQ
PLACE & TIME: 12.40 am

"A" Form.
MESSAGES AND SIGNALS.
Army Form C. 2121.

Prefix .... Code .... m.	Words	Charge	This message is on a/c of:	Recd. at 12.19 A m.
Office of Origin and Service Instructions.	Sent			Date A.W. 17.4.16
	At .... m.		........Service.	From A.W.C.
	To		(Signature of "Franking Officer.")	By Dinnen
	By			

TO — H Q

| Sender's Number. | Day of Month. | In reply to Number. | A A A |
| * | ~~MCH~~ 18TH | | |

All Quiet aaa left Coy
12.15 AM
1.4 AM
H Q 18 aaa
enemy snipers active along
whole of our front from 12.25
AM until 12.40 AM aaa all
Quiet now

left Coy 1.15 AM

From
Place
Time

"A" Form.
MESSAGES AND SIGNALS.

Army Form C. 2121.

Prefix	Code	Words	Charge	This message is on a/c of:	Recd. at m.
Office of Origin and Service Instructions. AWC		Sent		Service.	Date
		At m.			From
		To		(Signature of "Franking Officer.")	By
		By			

TO — H P DBS

Sender's Number.	Day of Month.	In reply to Number.	AAA
	15th		

Situation unchanged wind
north west—

From: C Coy DBS
Place:
Time:

The above may be forwarded as now corrected.   (Z)

Censor.   Signature of Addressor or person authorised to telegraph in his name.

* This line should be erased if not required.

"A" Form.　　　　　　　　　　　Army Form C. 2121.
MESSAGES AND SIGNALS.　　　No. of Message ....

TO: H Q D 3 5

Day of Month: 18th

AAA

Officer coming off duty at 12 midnight reports all quiet

From: O C B Coy

"A" Form.
MESSAGES AND SIGNALS.

TO: H 4 DBS

Patrol has apparently been observed as flares and a few rifle shots have been sent in their direction

From: O C B Co

Forster 20 men to Poplar.
will be followed at same
interval by Gordon Ralph
with 40 men who will extend
to left on reaching Forster's
party — Bacy to send
10 ofr + 20 men to Poplar

Gordon Ralph + extend to
his left when he extends
+ cover his left.

R. H. Hram p~~ostic on left~~
2. Battery train Evans + Elba

"A" Form.   Army Form C.2121.
MESSAGES AND SIGNALS.

Prefix	Code	m.	Words	Charge	This message is on a/c of:	Recd. at
Office of Origin and Service Instructions.						Date
			Sent		............Service.	From
			At........m.			
			To........			By
			By........		(Signature of "Franking Officer.")	

TO { H Q

Sender's Number.	Day of Month.	In reply to Number.	A A A

patrol right coy re
Lieut. Forester going out

From: O C C Coy
Place:
Time:

The above may be forwarded as now corrected. (Z)

Censor.   Signature of Addressor or person authorised to telegraph in his name.
* This line should be erased if not required.

"C" Form (Original).
MESSAGES AND SIGNALS.

Army Form C. 2123

Prefix SM Code FPM Words 43	Received From	Sent, or sent out At 9.45 P.m.	Office Stamp
AW £ s. d. Charges to collect	By	To B Coy	AW 17.4.18
Service Instructions		By Runner	

Handed in at .... Office .... m. Received .... m.

TO O.C. B Coy

*Sender's Number	Day of Month	In reply to Number	AAA
D3	17		

Warn Lieut FORSTER to get into position with his men in the vicinity of the POPLAR by 11 pm aaa Capt Gordon Ralph will have his patrol out about 11.30 pm aaa Acknowledge

Acknowledged

FROM
PLACE & TIME   C.O.

"C" Form (Duplicate).
MESSAGES AND SIGNALS.

Army Form C. 2123.
No. of Message ....

SM 1.6PM 37

Service Instructions.
A W

Charges to Pay.
9.29PM
AWB
Dinner

Office Stamp
AW
17.4.16

Handed in at .... Office .... m. Received .... m.

TO O.C B. Coy

Sender's Number: D2
Day of Month: 17
In reply to Number:
AAA

Warn Lieut GRANT to meet Capt Gordon Ralph with his party for the left at trench end of CRAWL BOYS ANE at 10.45 pm aaa acknowledge aaa.

Acknowledge

FROM C.O.
PLACE & TIME

"C" Form (Duplicate).
MESSAGES AND SIGNALS.

Army Form C. 2123.

SM1DX
AW 58

Service Instructions.

Charges to Pay. £ s. d.

Davies

Office Stamp
9.31

Handed in at .... Office .... m. Received .... m.

TO: Rifle Brigade

Sender's Number	Day of Month	In reply to Number	
	17		AAA

Will have a patrol out towards enemy's new work at the Z at 11.30 pm tonight aaa Can you kindly arrange to have a patrol to cover my left flank on the HANNESCAMPS — ESSART Road about E 17 9. 2 about

FROM
PLACE & TIME

"C" Form (Original). Army Form C. 2123
MESSAGES AND SIGNALS. No. of Message ....

Prefix ...... Code .... Words	Received	Sent, or sent out	Office Stamp
£ s. d.	From	At .... m.	
Charges to collect	By	To	
Service Instructions.		By	

Handed in at .... Office .... m. Received .... m.

TO — II

| *Sender's Number | Day of Month | In reply to Number | AAA |

11 pm aaa. Will inform you when your patrol is no longer required aaa

FROM DB5
PLACE & TIME

"C" Form (Duplicate).
MESSAGES AND SIGNALS.

Army Form C. 2123.

Service Instructions: SM IPPM 46 AW

Charges to Pay: All Coys

Office Stamp: 9.39 PM AW 17.4.16 Dinner

TO All Companies

Day of Month: 17

AAA

Capt Gordon Ralph with a patrol of 30 men will be in the vicinity of road running NE from POPLAR in front of enemys new work at Z at about 11.30 pm aaa Warn the right the same

FROM: C O

"C" Form (Original). Army Form O.2123
MESSAGES AND SIGNALS. No. of Message..........

Prefix **SM** Code **LKI** Words **10** Received From......... Sent, or sent out At.........m. Office Stamp.
Charges to collect **AX** By......... To.........
Service Instructions By **Le Davis Lt**

Handed in at................ Office.........m. Received **9.45** m.

| TO | D B 5 | | | |

*Sender's Number	Day of Month	In reply to Number.	AAA
RB441	17		
all	is	arranged	

FROM **D B 1**
PLACE & TIME **9.40 Pm**

"C" Form (Original).
MESSAGES AND SIGNALS.
Army Form C. 2123
No. of Message.............

Prefix SM	Code LP	Words 21	Received	Sent, or sent out	Office Stamp.
AX £ s. d. Charges to collect			From	At m.	
Service Instructions			By	By	

Handed in at .... Office .... m. Received 10/1 m.

TO   D B 5

Sender's Number	Day of Month	In reply to Number.	AAA
RB 551	17		

Please notify right company
d b 1 when all is over
aaa in addition to
d B 1.

FROM
PLACE & TIME   D B 1 9.55

"C" Form (Duplicate).
MESSAGES AND SIGNALS.   Army Form C. 2123

SM KBX 14
AMB

Service Instructions

Handed in at _____ Office _____ m. Received 10/19 m.

TO   D B 5

Sender's Number	Day of Month	In reply to Number.	AAA
AMB 185	17		

Your message re patrol asking
acknowledged

FROM
PLACE & TIME   LEFT Batln

War Diary

SECRET.   Copy No...1..........

2nd Battalion THE ROYAL IRISH REGIMENT.

ORDER NO. 11.

Ref. Trench Map Sheet 57d.N-E   4th April 1916.

---

1.   The Battalion will relieve the 1/East Lancashire Regiment in the Right Sector on the evening of the 5th instant.

2.   Companies will leave POMMIER in the following order -

                    A   D   B   C
                    C. B. D. C.

            The leading platoon of A Company will march off at 7 p.m. followed by other platoons at 5 minutes interval.

3.   Guides from 1/East Lancs will meet Platoons as under -

                                1 platoon A
            C & D Coys - Trench Hdqrs   - FONQUEVILLERS.
            A & B Coys - Crucifix   - HANNESCAMPS.
            (less 1 platoon)

4.   Companies will hold the line as under -

                    Right   -   D Coy.
                    Centre   -   A Coy.
                    Left   -   B Coy.
                    Support -   C Coy.

5.   Lewis Rifle Detachment and Signallers will take over at an hour to be notified later.

6.   One blanket per man and a W.P.Sheet will be carried on the man.

7.   Officers' Trench Kits will be stacked outside the Orderly Room by 5.30 p.m.

8.   All surplus blankets, Baggage, etc., will be stacked by 6 p.m., under a Guard to be detailed by QrMr at the CHURCH, POMMIER.   This will be removed by Regimental Transport as opportunity offers.

9.   Battalion Headquarters will close at POMMIER at 7.30 p.m. and re-open at FONQUEVILLERS at the same hour.

                        (sgd.)   T.A.LOWE   Capt. & Adjt.
                                  2nd Bn. The Royal Irish Regt.

Issued at 2 p.m.

Copy No. 1 - War Diary.   Copy No. 6 - O/C. 1/East Lancs.
     "   2 - O/C. A Coy.   "   7 - Transport Officer
     "   3 - O/C. B Coy.   "   8 - Machine Gun Officer.
     "   4 - O/C. C Coy.   "   9 - Medical Officer.
     "   5 - O/C. D Coy.

Copy No...1...

2nd Bn. THE ROYAL IRISH REGIMENT.

Order No. 12 - 10th April 1916.

Ref. Sh. 1:10,000 - FONQUEVILLERS.

---

1. The Battalion will be relieved in the trenches tomorrow by the 1/East Lancashire Regt.

2. Upon relief, companies will move into close support at FONQUEVILLERS AND HANNESCAMPS respectively as under -

   "A" & "C" Companies - FONQUEVILLERS.
   "B" & "D" Companies - HANNESCAMPS.
   Battn. Hdqrs will be at BIENVILLERS.

3. When relieved, companies will move out as under -

   (a) Support to FONQUEVILLERS via ROBERTS AVENUE.
   (b) Left to HANNESCAMPS via CHISWICK AVENUE.
   (c) Left CENTRE to FONQUEVILLERS via LA BRAYELLE ROAD
       Right CENTRE to FONQUEVILLERS via RED ROSE AVENUE.
   (d) Right to HANNESCAMPS via RED ROSE AVENUE - Communication trench FONQUEVILLERS-HANNESCAMPS.

   Coy Qtr Mtr Sgts will take over billets for their respective companies during daylight at FONQUEVILLERS AND HANNESCAMPS.

4. Lewis Guns Signallers and Grenade Officer will be relieved at 4 p.m.

5. Capt. MOORE-BRABAZON will command the detachment at FONQUEVILLERS and Capt. GORDON-RALPH will command the detachment at HANNESCAMPS.

6. Companies will report by wire to Battn Hdqrs when they have taken over at FONQUEVILLERS AND HANNESCAMPS.

7. Battn Hdqrs will close at FONQUEVILLERS at 9.30 p.m. and will open at BIENVILLERS at the same hour.

(sgd.) T. A. LOWE,   Capt.& Adjt.,

2nd Bn. The Royal Irish Regt.

Issued at..7.p.m...

Copy No. 1 - War Diary.   Copy No. 6 - Transport Officer.
  "   2 - O/C "A" Coy.   "   7 - Medical Officer.
  "   3 - " "B" "   "   8 - Lewis Rifle Officer.
  "   4 - " "C" "   "   9 - O/C 1/E.Lancs (for infn.)
  "   5 - " "D" "

Copy No. 1

2nd Battalion, THE ROYAL IRISH REGIMENT.

Order No. 13 - 16/4/16.

Ref. Trench Map, Fonquevillers, 57d N:E, 1:10,000

1.	The Battalion will relieve the 1st Bn, EAST LANCASHIRE REGT. in the Right Sector, tomorrow, 17th instant.

2.	Companies will occupy the line as under -

	Right - "C" Coy.
	Centre - "B" Coy.
	Left - "A" Coy.
	Support - "D" Coy.

3. RELIEF. "A" Company will leave FONQUEVILLERS at 7 p.m. and proceed to the Left via CRAWL BOYS LANE.
	"B" Company will leave HANNESCAMPS at 7.10 p.m. and proceed to the Centre via communication trench HANNESCAMPS-FONQVRS and CRAWL BOYS LANE.
	As soon as ONE Company of the 1/Somerset Light Infy has taken over at FONQUEVILLERS & HANNESCAMPS respectively, "C" Coy and "D" Coy will move as follows -
	"C" Coy to the right via RED NOSE AVENUE
	"D" Coy into Support via FONQUEVILLERS.

4.	Os/C Detachments at HANNESCAMPS & FONQUEVILLERS will arrange for all stores, ammunition and guards etc., to be handed over to detachments of the 1/Somerset Light Infy.

5.	The Battalion Bomb Officer will take over bombs in the line during daylight.
	Signallers, Lewis Rifles and H.Q.Guards will relieve those of the 1/East Lancs at 5.30 p.m.

6.	Officers spare kits will be dumped under charge of 1 man per detachment at Detachment H.Q. at HANNESCAMPS & FONQUEVILLERS H.Q. Officers kits will be dumped outside H.Q.Guard, BIENVILLERS, under charge of an Orderly. These will be brought back to ST AMAND by returning transport.

7.	Battalion H.Q. will close at BIENVILLERS at 7.30 p.m. and re-open at FONQUEVILLERS at the same hour.

	(Sgd.) T.A.LOWE,
		Capt. & Adjt.

	2nd Battn. The Royal Irish Regt.

Issued at... 6 p.m.

Copy No. 1 - War Diary   Copy No. 8 - Med. Offr.
 "   " 2 - O/C "A" Coy.   "   " 9 - Lewis Rif. Offr.
 "   " 3 - O/C "B" Coy.   "   " 10 - O/C S.L.I. for infn.
 "   " 4 - O/C "C" Coy.   "   " 11 - O/C E.L.   "
 "   " 5 - O/C "D" Coy.   "   " 12 - Battn Bomb Offr.
 "   " 6 -   Sen.Maj.   "   " 13 - Sergt-Maj.
 "   " 7 - Transport Offr.   "   " 14 - Signals.

S E C R E T.   Copy No........1...

SPECIAL ENTERPRISE BY TROOPS HOLDING THE RIGHT SECTOR AGAINST
ENEMY'S NEW WORK RUNNING NORTH EASTERLY FROM THE "Z" THROUGH
K.23.c & d.
----

1. PATROLS.
   (i) The 2nd Royal Irish Regt. will send out a strong patrol
   of 100 men under Capt. P.J.G.Gordon-Ralph, to move against
   the enemy's work with the following objectives:-
   (a) To capture any enemy's patrol in the vicinity; to drive
   in any enemy's covering party; to damage the enemy's wire
   in the vicinity of his work.
   This patrol will move into position via the HANNESCAMPS -
   LA BRAYELLE road, and when clear of our trenches will
   deploy to its left on a line parallel to the road running
   in a N.E. direction from the POPLAR to K.17.d.9.1., with
   its right resting on the HANNESCAMPS - LA BRAYELLE road.
   This patrol will be in position by 9-30 p.m. and will advance
   on its objective at 10 p.m.

   (ii) The 1st Bn. Somerset.L.I. will arrange for a patrol to
   cover the left flank of the Royal Irish patrol and to take
   up a position on the HANNESCAMPS - ESSARTS road in K.17.c.9.9.
   This patrol will be in position by 8-30 p.m.

   (iii) The 1st Bn. East Lancashire Regt. will cover the right
   of the Royal Irish patrol with a patrol in the rifle pits in
   the vicinity of the POPLAR. This patrol will be in
   position by 8-30 p.m.

2. ARTILLERY.
   The 27th Battery R.F.A. will fire intermittent fire on the
   enemy's new work from 8 p.m. to 10-15 p.m. In case the
   patrol is attacked this battery and the 134th Battery will
   put a barrage on enemy front line trenches from the "Little
   Z" to K.23.b.9.2.

3. LEWIS RIFLES.
   One at the POPLAR and one at the SOUTH FORTIN under orders
   of O.C. 1st East Lancashire Regt. One with the left party
   of the Royal Irish patrol under orders of Officer Commanding
   Patrol.

4. COMMUNICATIONS.
   O.C. 1st East Lancashire Regt. will lay out the following
   wires:-   1 to the POPLAR and 1 to follow the Royal Irish
   patrol. The left patrol (Somerset L.I.) will be connected
   by wire with Hd.Qrs. Left Sector.

5. WITHDRAWAL.
   Patrols will withdraw by the same road as which they went out.
   The patrols covering the flanks will not retire until the
   Royal Irish patrol is reported clear. Orders to that
   effect will be issued from Trench Hd.Qrs., FONQUEVILLERS.

6. HEADQUARTERS.
   Advanced Headquarters of the Royal Irish will be established
   at FONQUEVILLERS at 8 p.m., where all messages are to be sent.

                                                Lieut-Colonel,
16-4-16.   Commanding

Copies to:- No1 2nd. R.I.R.; No 2 1st Som.L.I.; No.3 1st E.Lan.R.
No 4 27th Battery R.F.A.; No 5 134th Battery R.F.A.; No 6 11th Bde HQ;
No 7 8th War. Regt.; No 8 Bde.M.G.Coy.; No 9 R.I.Det. Lewis Gun;
No 10 East Lancs. Lewis Gun Det.; No 11 File.

Issued 6 p.m.

2nd Bn. THE ROYAL IRISH REGIMENT.

PATROL REPORT - Night 16th/17th.

H.Q.,
11th Infy Brigade,

I beg to report that a special patrol consisting of 3 Officers and 100 men of the Battalion under my command, left our lines last night at 10 p.m. to reconnoitre enemy's new work enclosed by wire extending from "The Z" in a north-easterly direction through E.23.c.& d.

The first objective of this patrol was the road running from the vicinity of the POPLAR in a north-easterly direction to its junction with the HANNESCAMPS-ESSARTS Road at E.17.d.9.2. The flanks of the patrol were covered as follows:-

On the Right: By a patrol of the East Lancs at the POPLAR.
On the Left: By a patrol of the Som.L.I. in the sunken road about E.17.c.9.8.

These two latter patrols were in position by 8.30 p.m.

Up to 10.15 p.m., the 27th Battery R.F.A. had been firing intermittently on the enemy's new works in the vicinity of the "Z", and on his trenches north of it.

The patrol advanced in echelon formation with its left thrown back and with its right on the HANNESCAMPS-LA BRAYELLE ROAD. The night was particularly quiet and there was no firing from the enemy's trenches. The moon was somewhat obscured by clouds and a drizzling rain rather favoured our movements.

At 10.55 p.m. the patrol reached the road above referred to running N-E from the POPLAR to the HANNESCAMPS-ESSARTS ROAD without having encountered any enemy patrols or covering, and apparently without having been observed. The patrol took up a position in this road for some little time and sent forward small patrols towards the enemy's new wire to examine it. On receiving reports from these small patrols that no enemy were in the vicinity of the wire and that all appeared quiet the whole patrol (less a small covering party left in the road) advanced to the enemy's wire and began to cut it.

A lane was cut through the wire and the party proceeded through this lane to the enemy's side to reconnoitre. This party came across a small dump of wiring materials, from which they removed the following stores, -

15 iron stakes,
3 large rolls of barbed wire.
1 small roll partly used.
Some tracing tapes and pegs.
4 bombs which were found lying on the ground.

At 12 midnight the patrol withdrew and eventually rejoined our lines without casualty. The two patrols t covering the right and left flanks were ordered to withdraw as soon as the main patrol had rejoined our line.

Communications were maintained by means of a special wire, and a party of signallers which accompanied our patrol as well as by wire which were laid out to flanking patrols. These were connected up with advanced H.Q. established at FONQUEVILLERS for the occasion.

Arrangements

-2-

Arrangements had been made with the 32nd Brigade R.F.A. that in case of attack the 27th and 134th Batteries were to open Barrage Fire on the enemy's lines from the little "Z" to the trenches at, E.23.b.9.2.

Alltt Although this patrol did not meet with the success which it expected, viz., the capture of an enemy's patrol of covering party, I wish to bring to notice the very able manner in which it was handled by its commander Captain Gordon-Ralph, and also the intelligence displayed by all ranks concerned in keeping up communication throughout the patrol, and in the free way in which they moved across a somewhat difficult bit of country, exposed in places to the enemy's view on a moonlight night.

I would also like to bring to the notice of the Brigadier the able assistance and co-operation given me by the 1/Som.L.I. and the 1/E.Lancs who did everything they could to ensure the success of the operation.

Lieut-Col.,

17/4/16.   Comdg 2nd Bn. THE ROYAL IRISH REGT.

S E C R E T.

Copy No 10

2nd Bn. THE ROYAL IRISH REGIMENT.

Order no. 14 - 22/4/16.

Reference Sheet 57dN-E 1,10,000 (FONQUEVILLERS)

---

1. The Battalion will be relieved tomorrow, 23rd instant, by the 1st Bn. Hampshire Regt.

2. Upon relief, companies will move indepently direct by platoons to POMMIER, and take up billets there as allotted.

3. Companies will supply one guide per platoon, for the 1st Hants. They will report to Battalion Hdqrs at 7 p.m. for instructions.

4. Officers commanding companies will hand over to incoming companies, 1st Hants, list of work carried out and proposed.

5. When relieved, companies will move out as under:-

   (a) Support via ROBERTS AVENUE-FONQUEVILLERS-BIENVILLERS Road.
   (b) Left via HANNESCAMPS - LA BRAYELLE Road, HANNESCAMPS-BIENVILLERS.
   (c) Centre via LA BRAYELLE Road, FONQUEVILLERS, BIENVILLERS.
   (d) Right. via RED NOSE AVENUE FONQUEVILLERS, BIENVILLERS.

   C.Q.M.Ss and 1 guide per platoon will proceed to POMMIER at 3 p.m. and take over billets there for their respective companies. Lewis guns, signallers and Bomb Officer will be relieved at 4 p.m.

6. Officers trench kits will be dumped at Hdqrs FONQUEVILLERS, and at ration dump HANNESCAMPS by 7 p.m. The Transport Officer will make arrangements to take these to POMMIER, also to send Officers valises direct there in daylight from ST AMAND. C.Q.M.Ss will take these over at POMMIER. The R.S.M. will arrange for the Battalion Hdqr kits to be taken over.

7. Battalion Hdqrs will close at FONQUEVILLERS at 10 p.m. and will open at POMMIER at same hour.

(sd.) T. A. LOWE,

Capt & Adjt.

Issued at 7 p.m.   2nd Bn. The Royal Irish Regt.

Copy No.		Copy No.	
1	War Diary	7	Medical Officer.
2	O/C "A" Coy	8	Lewis Rifle Officer
3	O/C "B" Coy	9	O/C 1/Hants for infn.
4	O/C "C" Coy	10	R.S.M.
5	O/C "D" Coy	11	Signallers.
6	Trans Offr.		

2nd. Bn. The Royal Irish Regt.
Order No 15.

Reference Trench Map FONQUEVILLERS   The Field
Sheet 1:10000   28-4-16

1. The Battalion will relieve the 1/HAMPSHIRE RGT. in the RIGHT SECTOR.

2. Companies will occupy the line as under:-
   RIGHT   "B" COY.
   CENTRE   "A" "
   LEFT   "D" "
   SUPPORT   "C" "

3. Companies will leave POMMIER at the following hours (5 minutes interval between platoons):-

   "D" Coy 6.40 pm Route BIENVILLERS-HANNESCAMPS-CHISWICK AVENUE.

   "C" Coy 7 pm Route BIENVILLERS-FONQUEVILLERS-SNIPER'S SQUARE.

   "B" Coy 7.20 pm Route BIENVILLERS-FONQUEVILLERS-RED NOSE AVENUE.

   "A" Coy 7.40 pm Route BIENVILLERS-FONQUEVILLERS-CRAWL BOYS' LANE.

   N.B. The above time may be put back if enemy's Balloons are up before dusk.

4. The Battalion Bomb Officer will take over bombs in the line during daylight.
   Signallers, Lewis Rifles, and H.Q. Guard will relieve those of the 1/HAMPSHIRE RGT at 6. pm.

5. Officers' valises will be dumped outside the Orderly Room POMMIER by 12 noon. Trench kits at the same place by 7 pm.

6. Battalion Hdqr. will close at POMMIER at 7.30 pm and will reopen at FONQUEVILLERS at the same hour.

                Sd. T.A. LOWE, CAPT., & ADJT.,
                    2/ THE ROYAL IRISH REGT.

Issued at 7 pm
COPY No 1 War Diary   COPY No. 7 Medical Off.
  "   2 O/C "A" Coy.   "   8 Lewis Rifle Off.
  "   3 O/C "B" "   "   9 Quartermaster
  "   4 O/C "C" "   " 10 O/C 1/HANTS (for info)
  "   5 O/C "D" "   " 11 C.E. 10
  "   6 Trench Off   " 12 Signallers

11th Brigade
4th Division.

BATTALION TRANSFERRED TO 22nd BRIGADE
7th DIVISION 22nd MAY 1 9 1 6.

2nd BATTALION

ROYAL IRISH REGIMENT

M A Y 1 9 1 6

Attached:- Daily Summaries.
Operation Orders.

WAR DIARY
INTELLIGENCE SUMMARY

Army Form C. 2118

2nd R. Welch Reg¹
Vol 17 VII

Joined 22nd Brigade,
22nd May 1916.

Place	Date	Summary of Events and Information	Remarks and references to Appendices
Pernes-Villes	2/5	2nd R.W.F. Regt - arrived SOURCHE	No 16
Sourche	3		No 17
Hallry	4		
	5	Our class continues to receive ink and receive his share of hose passes and parades conducted in camp for same manner	Reinforcements
Berneville	6	2nd	No 18
		Lieut J.K. BERRY RFC joined the Bath - The R.W.F. him entertainment group in show war part - & other ranks joined the Bath	
		Transferred to CRAMONT	
Cramont	16th	Major J.G. GREGORIC joined the Bath - Bath continued farther training - some	No 19
		Orders received that the Battn. transferred 67th Division	
	21st	Marched to BERNAVILLE	No 20
Bernaville	2/5	Marched to LAVICOGNE - Prior't moved troops formed the KING'S LIVERPOOLS	No 21
Lavicogne	22nd	Marched to MOLLIANCOURT	No 22
Molliancourt	23	Arrived 6 p.m. having done 10 miles forced exceeding hot weather - met by Magnified of 22nd Brigade - 7th Division	
	25	Capt. Hon. H.A.V. PRESTON, V. RHODES, I.J. LITTLE, E.E. HODGES joined the Bath	
	29	5 a.m. Marched to - Camp BOIS DESTROCES	No 23 (2 sheets)

WAR DIARY
INTELLIGENCE SUMMARY

Army Form C. 2118

2 R Irish Regt
No 17 VII B

Place	Date	Hour	Summary of Events and Information	Remarks and references to Appendices
PONT REMY	2/9		Relieved by 2nd Battn EAST LANCASHIRE REGT - and proceeded SOUASTRE	"No 16 No 17
SOUASTRE	3	10 am	Marched to HALLOY	
HALLOY	4		2 Lieut HARRISON joined the Battn.	Relief
"	5		No 8186 Pte J. ALFORD joined unit. Our C.O. awarded 6 months I.H.L. and without hard labor suspension of sentence for his prompt and plucky conduct in a misfire from firm training.	No 18
		8 am	Marched to BERNAVILLE and arrived in Burade.	
BERNAVILLE	6		Lieut J. BERRY M.C. joined the Battn. The Battn. here entrained Troops in your airful.	
			2.Lieuts. Smith joined the Battn	
"	12		Marched to CRAMONT	No 19
CRAMONT	18th		Major L. GREGORIE joined the Battn. Battn reviewed under Brigade arrangements.	
	&		Officer received per the Battn transferred 61st Division	
	19th		Marched to BERNAVILLE	
BERNAVILLE	21st		Marched to LA VICOGNE - Pres. & marched Major General to Hon. H.LAMBSTON	No 20 No 21
			and received the Battn.	
LA VICOGNE	22nd		Marched to MIRLANCOURT	No 22
MIRLANCOURT	22nd		Arrived 6 p.m. having done 19 mile march excepting last seventh - met by	
			Brigadier of 2 R.D. Int Brigade - 7th Division.	
	23		Capt & Hon. H.A.V. PRESTON & 2Lieuts J.J. LITTLE - E.E. HODGES joined the Battn.	
	28	5 pm	Marched to Camp BOIS DESTRILLES -	No 23

5.B.
25 April

Army Form C. 2118.

WAR DIARY
or
INTELLIGENCE SUMMARY.
(Erase heading not required.)

Instructions regarding War Diaries and Intelligence Summaries are contained in F.S. Regs., Part II. and the Staff Manual respectively. Title pages will be prepared in manuscript.

Place	Date	Hour	Summary of Events and Information	Remarks and references to Appendices
Bois DES HULLUS	26th	6pm	Arrived -	Appendix No 1
C2 Sub Sector	27th		Proceeded from Bois DES HULLUS to C2 Sub Sector to relieve 2nd Bn R. WARWICKSHIRE Regt in the trenches.	No. 24
"	28th		8o. Mr. ranks wounded in action.	
"	30th		2nd Lt B FORSTER & Rank Scouts carried out very useful work	
"	31st		1 other rank wounded in action. Lt MURPHY joined the Battn	

Ou Sergeg
CAPTAIN & ADJ...
2nd BATTN: THE ROYAL IRISH REGT.

2nd. Battalion The Royal Irish Regiment.

DAILY SUMMARY. 28/5/16.

1. OPERATIONS.   - Nil -

2. INTELLIGENCE.
   Enemy's activity:-
      Artillery.   Heavy guns shelled hill right of KINGSTON RD.
         4 small shells fell in the vicinity of RAILWAY AVENUE at
         dusk.
      Trench Mortars.   Active right of KINGSTON RD. One
         fell into wire in C2 Sector at "stand to" yesterday
         evening.
      Machine Guns.   Active during night.
   Patrols:-   A patrol out from "stand to" yesterday evening
      to dawn this morning had nothing of importance to report
      except that a large enemy working party to the right of
      AEROPLANE TRENCH was dispersed by our Lewis Gun fire.
   Miscellaneous:-   Enemy automatic gun or rifle replied to
      our Lewis Gun fire on WICKED CORNER from point of "V" in
      WICKED CORNER

3. PROGRESS OF WORK.
   Trenches 5 to 16 cleaned and bays revetted. Alternative
   positions from which Lewis Guns may fire selected. Deepening
   new trench at 71 NORTH. Work on new parados left of 71 NORTH
   commenced.

The Field.   Lieut. Colonel,
28/5/16.   Commdg. 2nd. Battalion The Royal Irish Regiment.

War Diary

copy

Duplicate to Hdts

War Diary

2nd. Battalion The Royal Irish Regiment.

DAILY SUMMARY.   29/5/16.

1. OPERATIONS.   -Nil-

2. INTELLIGENCE.

   Enemy's activity:-

   Artillery.   C2 Sector shelled with heavies between 5.45 p.m. and 6.15 p.m. 84 Street damaged. Twice during night groups of 4 were fired from enemy field guns followed by violent m.g. fire along whole front. BARRIER 4 Shell fell from 11.45a

   Trench Mortars.   A few mortars fell into the CEMETRY during the night. Active from 7.45 p.m. to 9 p.m.

   Signals.   Red flare from WICKED CORNER was followed by violent machine gun fire.

   Patrol.   A patrol of 1 Officer and 11 other ranks reported on 27th. inst., - Large working party at work on enemy's front line left of AEROPLANE TRENCH. This was dispersed by our Lewis gun fire. Sniper observed firing from centre of AEROPLANE TRENCH and this trench was entered by our patrol and bombed. No retaliation. Enemy on the alert. Machine Gun fired from left sap of AEROPLANE TRENCH. No wire found in the SUNKEN ROAD opposite F.9.2.

   A patrol of 1 officer and 10 other ranks reported on the night 28th. inst., - Enemy party working on trenches left of AEROPLANE TRENCH also wiring party at that point. These parties were dispersed by our Lewis Gun fire. Trucks heard on enemy's trench railway at 10.40 p.m. Enemy sent up red flare at 11.45 p.m. At 12.30 a.m. patrol was within 40 yards of SUNKEN ROAD. 2 large enemy parties were seen on either flank. Patrol withdrew to within 50 yards of our wire. A new German bomb and an old French rifle were discovered.

3. PROGRESS OF WORK.

   RAILWAY AV. S.   Trench boards levelled and sumps cleaned.
   RAILWAY AV. N.   Trench cleaned in the vicinity of water tank.
   85 STREET.   Bridge traverse built. Parados and parapets improved and heightened. A new sap started and proceeded with. a disused sap being reopened
   KINGSTON ROAD.   Trench deepened in several places and revetting carried out. Cleaning up and removing earth from blown in dug-out. Making sniper's pits. One fire step revetted and one partially revetted.

The Field.   Lieut. Colonel,
29/5/16.   Commanding 2nd. Battalion The Royal Irish Regiment.

War Diary

2nd. Battalion The Royal Irish Regiment.

DAILY SUMMARY 30/5/16.

1. OPERATIONS.   -Nil-

2. INTELLIGENCE.
   Enemy's activity:-
   Artillery.   Artillery less active than usual. MAPLE REDOUBT was heavily shelled about 6.30 p.m. yesterday evening.
   Trench Mortars.   A few trench mortars fell into the CEMETRY during the day.

   Patrols:-
   A patrol of eleven men under 2/Lt. T. B. Forster left our lines at 9.30 p.m. to reconnoitre the SUNKEN ROAD and enemy's trenches in the vicinity of the RECTANGLE and AEROPLANE TRENCH. Between 10 p.m. and midnight, the patrol reported a working party at F.9.B.5.4. This party was dispersed by our Lewis Gun fire. At 1.30 a.m. the scouts of the patrol occupied the SUNKEN ROAD opposite AEROPLANE TRENCH and discovered a patrol of the enemy. Fourteen bombs were thrown by our patrol the enemy replied with six hand grenades and then retired. Our patrol opened rapid fire and then 2/Lt. Forster and four men advanced to see if there were any enemy casualties but discovered none. The patrol followed up the enemy into the AEROPLANE TRENCH as far as the main trench the entrance to which was blocked with a knife rest and coiled wire. Our men threw four bombs into the trench and silenced a sniper who had been firing on our patrol. Our patrol withdrew at 2 a.m. and regained our lines without any casualties.

3. PROGRESS OF WORK.
   Snipers posts constructed. Trench deepened. Dug-out, destroyed by shell fire, cleared and cleaned. Parapet and parados near destroyed dug-out repaired.
   Wiring across road and between SANDOWN AVENUE and RAILWAY AVENUE.
   Front line.- Advance trench improved, deepened, work on completion of traverses. Ordinary and communication trench improved. Wiring. Opening up new sap.

The Field.   Lieut. Colonel,
30/5/16.   Commanding 2nd. Battalion The Royal Irish Regiment.

War Diary

2nd. Battalion The Royal Irish Regiment.

DAILY SUMMARY. 31/5/16.

1. OPERATIONS.   - Nil -

2. INTELLIGENCE.
   Enemy's activity:-

   Artillery.   Very active.
   C2 Sector bombarded between 5 p.m. and 6.30 p.m. A certain amount of immaterial damage was done to our trenches. First and second line trenches were bombarded between 8.30 p.m. and 10 p.m. Work had to be suspended during this bombardment.

   Trench Mortars.   Trench mortars were fired into the CEMETRY from 5 p.m. to 6.30 p.m., at 7 p.m., and from 9.45 p.m. to 10.15 p.m.

   Machine Guns.   Great activity during the greater part of the night. Heavy fire at 2 a.m.

   Sniping.   Increased activity.

   Patrols.   2/Lt. T. B. Forster and his patrol left our lines at 9.50 p.m. to reconnoitre.
   Two hostile working parties were reported working on (a) AEROPLANE TRENCH and (b) THE RECTANGLE, both these parties were dispersed by our Lewis Gun fire. No hostile patrols were encountered.
   The patrol returned at daybreak. The enemy were very much on the alert throughout the night. Machine Guns were active and sniping was carried on all through the night. Our patrol was evidently expected by the enemy. One casualty was sustained, a chance shot breaking a man's arm.

3. PROGRESS OF WORK.
   Trenches cleared. Fire bays deepened and revetted with sandbags.
   SANDOWN AVENUE and ~~CEMETRY AVENUE~~ cleaned and deepened.

The Field.   Lieut. Colonel,
31/5/16.   Commanding 2nd. Battalion The Royal Irish Regiment.

19th May 1916

Dear Gregory,

I hear that your Battalion is leaving the 11th Brigade tomorrow and I take this opportunity of expressing on behalf of all ranks of the 1st East Lancashire Rt, our sincere regrets that the mutual good feeling & comradeship which exists between the two Battalions, should be temporarily in abeyance. We should have been delighted & proud to have fought alongside you in the near future, but Fate has decided otherwise and all that is left to us is to wish to the 2nd Bn Royal Irish Regiment the best of luck in your new Brigade, that you will certainly succeed in whatever you may be asked to undertake is the conviction of the 1st Bn East Lancashire Rt. Good bye & good luck to you all.

Yours sincerely

J. E. Green Lt Col
Comdg. 1st East Lancs
Rt

20th May
1916

My dear Dugan
             I write to express
my regret at the departure
of the 2nd Bn Royal Irish
Regiment from the 5th Div,
& to thank you & all ranks
for your good work during
the last 8 months.
Since the Battalion has
joined this Division its
conduct has been admirable,
its smartness on parade
excellent, & its work both

in the trenches & in billets done cheerfully & efficiently. I very much regret losing this battalion, which I feel sure will prove itself equally efficient in any fighting which may fall to its lot.

Yours sincerely
W Lambton

2nd Bn. The Royal Irish Regiment   Copy No 1.
          Order No. 16.
Reference Map. France - LENS. 11.   The Field
       1=100,000   1st May 1916.

---

1. The Battalion will be relieved in the Right Sector by the 8th Bn. E. Lancashire Regt. on the night 2/3 May.

2. On relief, Companies will proceed to SOUASTRE independently by platoons as under :-
   Right Company }
   Support   "   } FONQUEVILLERS — SOUASTRE.
   Centre Company }
   Left   "   } CRAWL BOYS' LANE — FONQUEVILLERS — SOUASTRE.

3. Companies will be relieved and will march out in the following order :- Left, Centre, Right, Support.

4. Companies will arrange for 1 guide per platoon to meet platoons of the 8th Bn. E. Lancashire Regt. as under. <u>An Officer per company will be in charge of each group of guides.</u> These Officers will accompany the last platoons into the line.
   Left Company — Barrier BIENVILLERS - HANNESCAMPS RD
                   (HANNESCAMPS end) 7.30 p.m.
   Platoons of this company will move into the line via CHISWICK AVENUE.
   Centre Company }
   Right   "   } at road junction BIENVILLERS -
   Support "   } FONQUEVILLERS RD (FONQUEVILLERS end)
                    7.45 p.m.

5. <u>Lewis Rifles, Signallers, Guards etc.</u>
   The Battalion Lewis Rifle Officer will arrange for guides to meet the incoming detachments at the FONQUEVILLERS and HANNESCAMPS barriers at 5.30 p.m.
   Signallers, H.Q. Guard etc will be relieved during daylight under arrangements to be made direct with the 8th Bn East Lancashire Regt.

6. <u>Trench Stores</u> — O's. C. Coys. will prepare a list of trench stores, ammunition etc. to be handed over to relieving companies. A duplicate list receipted by the incoming companies will be handed in at Battn H.Qrs. at FONQUEVILLERS as companies march out. The trench stores at Bn. H.Qrs. including Gum Boots will be
                                        /collected

collected by the Regtl. Sergeant Major who will prepare lists ready for handing over during daylight.

7. Very Pistols & Wire Cutters will NOT be handed over but will be retained by Companies.

8. Lewis Ammunition and Officers' Trench Kits etc
(a) Left Company will dump at HANNESCAMPS under a guard by 7 p.m.
(b) Right, Centre, Support Coy & Battn. H.Q. will dump outside Bn. Gr. Guard at FONQUEVILLERS by 7 p.m.

9. Transport. The Regtl. Transport Officer will arrange for ammunition and kits mentioned in para 8 above to be collected and brought to SOUASTRE. After off loading, transport will return to ST. AMAND. No transport of the Battalion will enter FONQUEVILLERS or HANNESCAMPS before 8.15 p.m. and must be clear of these villages by 9 p.m. Transport will be off loaded at SOUASTRE by H.Qr. Details.

10. Rations & Cookers. Rations for the 3rd inst. will be brought up to HANNESCAMPS and FONQUEVILLERS by incoming transport and loaded at the Company Cookers. These will proceed to SOUASTRE with returning transport.

11. Billeting Parties: The Quartermaster Sgt. of each company and one representative per platoon, the whole under an officer to be detailed by "C" Company will report to 2/Lt NEVILL at the Town Major's Office SOUASTRE at 5 p.m. to arrange billets for their companies. 2/Lt NEVILL will arrange billets for Bn. HQrs. This party will rendezvous at Battn. HQrs. FONQUEVILLERS at 2 p.m. and proceed to SOUASTRE via HANNESCAMPS and BIENVILLERS. These guides will meet their companies at the junction FONQUEVILLERS—SOUASTRE RD with the BIENVILLERS—SOUASTRE RD by 10.30 p.m. and will guide their platoons to their billets.

12. Battn. HQrs will close at FONQUEVILLERS at 11 p.m. and will re-open at SOUASTRE at the same hour.

    Sd. T. A. LOWE, CAPT. & ADJT.
    2/ THE ROYAL IRISH REGT.

Issued at 7 p.m.

Copy No 1. War Diary	No. 6. L.R. Off.	No. 11. R.S.M.
2. O/C "A" Coy	7. M/Off.	12. Sigs.
3. O/C "B" "	8. T. Off.	13. Interpreter
4. O/C "C" "	9. Q.M.	
5. O/C "D" "	10. O/C S/EL (for infor)	

2nd Bn. The Royal Irish Regiment   Copy No
Order No. 16.
Reference Map. France - LENS 11.   The Field
           1:100.000.   1st May 1916.

---

1. The Battalion will be relieved in the Right Sector by the 8th Bn. E. Lancashire Regt. on the night 2/3 May.

2. On relief Companies will proceed to SOUASTRE independently by platoons as under:-

   Right Company }
   Support   "   } FONQUEVILLERS — SOUASTRE.

   Centre Company } CRAWL BOYS' LANE — FONQUEVILLERS
   Left   "   } — SOUASTRE.

3. Companies will be relieved and will march out in the following order:- Left, Centre, Right, Support.

4. Companies will arrange for 1 guide per platoon to meet platoons of the 8th Bn E. Lancashire Regt. as under. <u>An Officer per company will be in charge of each group of guides.</u> These Officers will accompany the last platoons into the line.

   Left Company — Barrier BIENVILLERS - HANNESCAMPS RD (HANNESCAMPS end) 7.30 p.m.
   Platoons of this company will move into the line via CHISWICK AVENUE.

   Centre Company }
   Right   "   } at road junction BIENVILLERS -
   Support "   } FONQUEVILLERS RD (FONQUEVILLERS end)
                        7.45 p.m.

5. <u>Lewis Rifles, Signallers, Guards etc.</u>

   The Battalion Lewis Rifle Officer will arrange for guides to meet the incoming detachments at the FONQUEVILLERS and HANNESCAMPS barriers at 5.30 p.m.

   Signallers, H.Q. Guard etc will be relieved during daylight under arrangements to be made direct with the 8th Bn East Lancashire Regt.

6. <u>Trench Stores</u> — O.C. Coys will prepare a list of trench stores, ammunition, etc. to be handed over to relieving companies. A duplicate list receipted by the incoming companies will be handed in at Battn HQrs. at FONQUEVILLERS as companies march out. The trench stores at Bn. HQrs. including Gum Boots will be
   /collected

collected by the Regtl. Sergeant Major who will prepare lists ready for handing over during daylight.

7. Very Pistols & Wire Cutters will NOT be handed over but will be retained by Companies.

8. Lewis Ammunition and Officers' Trench Kits etc
(a) Left Company will dump at HANNESCAMPS under a guard by 7 p.m.
(B) Right, Centre, Support Coy & Battn HQ will dump outside Bn. Gr. Guard at FONQUEVILLERS by 7 p.m.

9. Transport. The Regtl. Transport Officer will arrange for ammunition and kits mentioned in para 8 above to be collected and brought to SOUASTRE. After off loading, transport will return to ST. AMAND. No transport of the Battalion will enter FONQUEVILLERS or HANNESCAMPS before 8.15 p.m. and must be clear of these villages by 9 p.m. Transport will be off loaded at SOUASTRE by H.Qr. Details.

10. Rations & Cookers. Rations for the 3rd inst. will be brought up to HANNESCAMPS and FONQUEVILLERS by incoming transport and loaded at the Company Cookers. These will proceed to SOUASTRE with returning transport.

11. Billeting Parties: The Quartermaster Sgt. of each company and one representative per platoon, the whole under an officer to be detailed by "C" Company will report to 2/Lt NEVILL at the Town Major's Office SOUASTRE at 5 p.m. to arrange billets for their companies. 2/Lt NEVILL will arrange billets for Bn. HQrs. This party will rendezvous at Battn. HQrs. FONQUEVILLERS at 2 p.m. and proceed to SOUASTRE via HANNESCAMPS and BIENVILLERS. These guides will meet their companies at the junction FONQUEVILLERS—SOUASTRE RD with the BIENVILLERS—SOUASTRE RD by 10.30 p.m. and will guide their platoons to their billets.

12. Battn. HQrs will close at FONQUEVILLERS at 11 p.m. and will re-open at SOUASTRE at the same hour

    Sd. T. A. LOWE, CAPT. & ADJT.
    2/ THE ROYAL IRISH REGT.

Issued at 7 p.m.

Copy No 1. War Diary   No. 6 L.R. Offr.   No. 11. R.S.M
 2. O/C "A" Coy.   7. M.O.ffr.   12. Sigs
 3. O/C "B" "   8. T. Offr.   13. Interpreter
 4. O/C "C" "   9. Q.M.
 5. O/C "D" "   10. O/C S/E.L.
      (for infn)

2nd. Bn. The Royal Irish Regiment   Copy No. 6
             Order No. 17.
                                                The Field
Reference Map LENS 11. 1/100,000   2nd May 1916

1. The Battalion will march to HALLOY (F 5) tomorrow. Route:- HENU – PAS – GRENAS.

2. Starting Point:- Road Junction ½ mile West of the H in HENU.

3. Companies will move to the starting point in the following order: C. D. B. A. "C" Company will leave SOUASTRE at 10 am. An interval of 5 minutes will be kept between companies en route to the starting point. On arrival at the Starting Point, Companies will fall out and await orders to move forward.

4. Transport. The Regimental Transport will be formed up on the ST AMAND – HENU Road clear of the starting point by 11 am.

5. Kits etc. Officers' Kits will be dumped outside the Battalion H.Q. Guard by 9 am. These will be loaded on a limber detailed by the Transport Officer. All other stores will be dumped at H.Q. Guard by 6.45 am. and will be loaded on a lorry. The loading of stores at ST AMAND will be carried out in accordance with special instructions issued to Transport Officer & Q.Master.

6. Advanced Party. Lt. McGrath, Coy. Q.M. Sgts. and one representative per platoon will parade at Battalion H.Q. at 7 am. and proceed to HALLOY to take over billets for the Battalion.

7. Reveillé 6.30 am, Breakfasts 8 am. Dinners on arrival at HALLOY. Company Cookers will follow 5 minutes in rear of "A" Coy to starting point and then join up with Transport when the Battalion moves forward.

                         Sd. T. A. LOWE, CAPT, & ADJT,
Issued at 3 pm.   2/ THE ROYAL IRISH REGIMENT.
Copy No.1. War Diary
     2. O/C "A" Coy   Copy No 6. Transport Off.
     3. O/C "B" Coy   7. Quartermaster.
     4. O/C "C" Coy   8. Medical Off.
     5. O/C "D" Coy   9. Lewis R. Off.
                              10. R.S.M.

SPECIAL ORDER

The Commanding Officer wishes the following order to be made known to all ranks:—

The Commander-in-Chief has been pleased to remit 6 months I.H.L. and has ordered the release in suspension of sentence of No 8186 Pte J. ALFORD, 2/The Royal Irish Regiment, (awarded 2 years I.H.L. on 4/8/15 for "Desertion") in view of his prompt & plucky conduct in saving a Frenchman from drowning.

The circumstances were as follows:—

On the 2/4/16 while this man was working on the banks of the Seine a French workman fell off a raft into the river in about 12 feet of water and at a place where there was a strong tide. Pte ALFORD threw himself into the water, clothed and it was only by repeated diving by this man that the Frenchman was found and brought to the bank.

Authy A.G. G.H.Q. B/4835 of 24/4/16.

30/4/16.

Sd. T.A. LOWE Capt. & Adjt,
2/The Royal Irish Regt.

BATTALION ORDERS
-by-
Lieut. Colonel W. J. Dugan D.S.O., Commanding
2nd Battn. The Royal Irish Regiment

No 119   Part — 1.   5-5-16.

1. **Orderly Officer**: Orderly Officer tomorrow 2/Lt. Stuttaford. Next for duty 2/Lt. Wynne.
2. **Duties**: Coy for duty tomorrow "C" Coy.
3. **Transfer**: No 5998 Pte. W. Collins transferred from "B" Coy to "C" Coy.
4. **Joinings**: No. 886 Pte. J. Alford joined the unit today and is posted to "B" Coy.
5. **Orders - Issue of**: Attention is drawn to Operation Order No. 18 issued at noon today.
6. **Return to duty**: No. 10795 Pte T. Meskill, "B" Coy. returns to duty from the Lewis Rifle Detachment.
7. ~~Correspondence with Strangers~~. G.R.O. 1551. 3/5/16.
   All ranks are cautioned against replying to trade circulars from unknown merchants ~~except~~ especially those belonging to neutral countries.
8. **Dress**. G.R.O. 1556 - 3/5/16. N.C.O's & men awarded the Military Medal are permitted to wear the riband as soon as the award of the medal has been notified.
9. **4th Divl. School of Instruction**: Owing to the move the arrangements for the next course are cancelled.

         Part — 2

1. **Reversion**. No 5998 Sgt. W. Collins reverts to private at his own request with effect from today.

         Sd. J. A. Lowe Capt & Adjt.
         2/ The Royal Irish Regt.

2nd BN. THE ROYAL IRISH REGT.
ORDER NO. 18.

Copy No. 1.

Reference map LENS. 11
Sheet 1/100,000

The Field
5-5-16

1. The Battalion will move to BERNAVILLE (C.50.5) tomorrow. Route AMPLIER – DOULLENS – HEM-FIENVILLERS.

2. Companies will be formed up in column of route in camp ready to march off at 7.40 am.
Transport will be hooked in in line on the present horse lines and will follow the Battalion. Companies will march in the following order:-
D. B. A. C.

3. The Battalion will halt for 2 hours for dinners.

4. Kits, Blankets & W.P. Sheets will be loaded up by 7 am.

5. Reveillé .... 5.30 am
   Breakfasts ...... 6.15 "

Sd. T.A. LOWE, CAPT, & ADJT,
2/ THE ROYAL IRISH REGT.

Issued at 12 noon

Copy No. 1. War Diary   Copy No. 6. L.R. Offr.
       2. O/C "A" Coy   7. Transpt. Offr.
       3. O/C "B" "   8. M.O.
       4. O/C "C" "   9. Offr i/c Scouts
       5. O/C "D" "   10. R.S.M.

SECRET.   Copy No. 5

        11th Infantry Brigade.   Operation Order No. 7.

    Reference Sheet II LENS 1/100,000.   5ᵗʰ May, 1916.

    1.   The Brigade, attached T.M.Batteries and 2 sections
    Durham Field Coy. R.E. will move from its present area on 6th inst.
    to area LONGVILLERS. BEAUMETZ. PROUVILLE. BERNAVILLE.
    VACQUERIE. GORGES.

    2.   The march will be carried out as a Brigade in accordance
    with the attached March Table.

    3.   1st Line Transport and Baggage Wagons will march in rear of
    Units.

    4.   Separate instructions are being issued as regards
    Billeting parties.

    5.   Acknowledge.

                                            _____
                                                   Captain.

                                       Brigade Major,
                                         11th Infantry Brigade.

    Issued at 9 a.m.

    Copies to :-

              1. 4th Division G.
              2. 4th Division Q.
              3. Detachment Durham R.E.
              4. Somerset L.Inf.
              5. Royal Irish.
              6. East Lancs.
              7. Hants.
              8. Rif. Bde.
              9. 11th Bde M.G.Coy.
              10. Y.4. T.M.Batty.
              11. 11/1 T.M.Batty.
              12. 11/2 T.M.Batty.
              13. Grenade School.
              14. File.

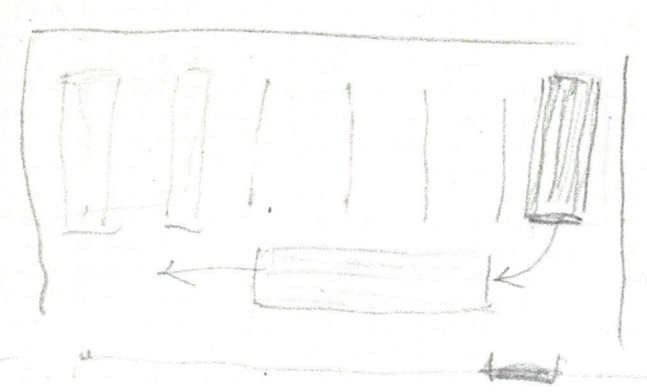

Reference LENS Sheet 11 1/100,000

	STARTING POINT.			
TROOPS	Place	Time of passing.	ROUTE	DESTINATION
Bde Hd Qrs No 3 Sig Section	Road junction just North of P in la Voie des Pres	9 am	DOULLENS HEM FIENVILLERS	BERNAVILLE
1/ Hants Regt.	"	9.5 am	" "	LONGVILLERS
1/ Somerset L.I.	"	9.10 am	" "	PROUVILLE
1/ Rifle Bde	L in B BRULE on Halloy - AMPLIER Road	8 am	AMPLIER DOULLENS HEM FIENVILLERS	BEAUMETZ
1/ East Lancs	"	8.5 am	"	BERNAVILLE
2/ Royal Irish	"	8.10 am	"	BERNAVILLE
11th Bde M.G. Coy Grenade School	Road junction just South of P in la Voie des Pres	9.30 am	DOULLENS HEM FIENVILLERS	GORGES
1/ 4 Sth. Batty 11/1 " 11/2 "	"	9.33 am	DOULLENS FIENVILLERS GORGES	VACQUERIE
2 Sections DURHAM R.E.	"	9.35 am	DOULLENS FIENVILLERS BERNAVILLE	BEAUMETZ

2nd Battn The Royal Irish Regiment   Copy No 1
Operation Order No 19

Reference Sheet 1/10000 LENS 11.   The Field 14th /16

1. The Battalion will move to CRAMONT tomorrow, route – BEAUMETZ – LONGVILLERS

2. Starting Point – Road junction BERNAVILLE – PROUVILLE, BERNAVILLE – BEAUMETZ Roads

3. Companies will be formed up in column of route at the starting point at 9.30 am. and will march in the following order –
      A. B. C. D.

4. The first line transport will march in rear of the Battalion.

5. All officer's kits and stores to be loaded up by 8 am.

6.   Reveillé — 6 am.
      Breakfasts — 7 am.

                  Sd. T. A. Lowe Captain & Adjt
                  2nd Bn The Royal Irish Regt

Hour of issue – 1 pm.

Copy No 1. War Diary   Copy No 6 Transpt Offr
      2 O/C "A" Coy   7 Lewis R.O.
      3   "   "B" "   8 R.M.
      4   "   "C" "   9 R.S.M.
      5   "   "D" "   10 Drums

2nd Battn. The Royal Irish Regt.   Copy No.
                Order No 20   The Field
Reference Map LENS Sheet 1/40.000   19-5-16
_____

1. The Battalion will move to BERNAVILLE (C.5 0 5) tomorrow.
   Route - LONGVILLERS — BEAUMETZ
   Starting Point — Last house on the right of the ORMONT - LONGVILLERS Road

2. Companies will be formed up in column of route at the starting point (time to be notified later) and will march in the following order —
   D. A. B. C

3. The first line transport will march in rear of the Battalion.

4. All officers' kits and stores to be loaded up by 8.30 am.

5. Reveille   5.30 am
   Breakfasts   7   am

                    Sd. I. A Lowe Capt & Adjt
                    2/The Royal Irish Regiment

Hour of issue — 9.30 pm.

Copy No 1 War Diary   No 6 Quartermaster
       2 O/C "A" Coy   7 Transpt Offr
       3   " "B" "   8 Lewis Off.
       4   " "C" "   9 R.S.M.
       5   " "D" "   10 Drums

2nd Battn. The Royal Irish Regt.   Copy No 1
        Operation Order No 21.

Reference Map LENS 11   The Field
        Sheet 1/100.000   20/5/16

1. The Battalion will move to LA VICOGNE tomorrow
   Route: FIENVILLERS — CANDAS — B of ANSN.
   MIN DE VALHEUREUX — VERT: GALAND F.14.

2. Starting Point:— Road junction immediately
   North of first E in BERNAVILLE

3. Order of March — A — B — C — D
   The Battalion will be formed up at the starting
   point at 8.30 a.m.
   The first line transport will march in rear of
   the Battalion.

4. An advance party under 2/Lieut NEVILLE will
   report to the Town Major, LA VICOGNE at
   9 a.m.

5. Reveillé 5.30 a.m., Breakfast 6.30 a.m.
   Sick Parade 7 a.m. Commanding Officers
   Orders one hour after arrival at LA
   VICOGNE.

6. Wagons to be packed by 8 a.m.

                        Sd. J. Lowe Capt & Adjt
                        2/The Royal Irish Regt.
Issued at 7.15 p.m.
Copies to —
    No 1 War Diary   No 6. Quartermaster
     2 O/C "A" Cy   7 Transpt Offr
     3   " "B" "   8 Lewis R Offr
     4   " "C" "   9 M.O
     5   " "D" "   10 R.S.M
                    11 Drums

B.M.797.

O.C. 2/Royal Irish Regt.

1. Your Battalion will march from BERNAVILLE to MORLANCOURT in accordance with attached March Table.

2. On arrival at MORLANCOURT your Battalion will come under orders of 7th Division.

3. (a) Supply Section will march with Battalion from BERNAVILLE carrying rations for consumption on the 22nd inst.

(b) Rations for consumption on 23rd will be delivered on the evening of 22nd at La VICOGNE by Lorry.

(c) Rations for consumption on 24th will be provided by 7th Division.

4. A 5 ton lorry will report at your H.Q. at BERNAVILLE at 7.30 a.m. on 22nd. and will take surplus Lewis Gun Ammn. and surplus kits direct to MORLANCOURT.

5. Acknowledge.

Captain.

Brigade Major,
11th Infantry Brigade.

HEAD QUARTERS
Date 20.5.16.
11th INFANTRY BRIGADE

MARCH TABLE. 2/ROYAL IRISH REGIMENT. Issued by. 11th INFANTRY BRIGADE.

Reference Sheet 11 LENS and Sheet 17. AMIENS.

Date.	From	To.	Time of start.	Route.	Remarks.
21st May.	BERNAVILLE	LA VICOGNE.	8.30 a.m.	FIENVILLERS, CANDAS, R. OF Ancre, Min. de VAUHEUREUX VERT-GALAND. Ma.	Battn. will billet in La VICOGNE for night 21-22. Billeting parties in advance report to Town Commandant.
22nd May.	LA VICOGNE	MORLANCOURT	5 a.m.	TALMAS, RUBEMPRE, BEHENCOURT, FRANVILLERS, HEILLY, HALTE, MERICOURT VILLE, SOUL CORBIE.	A halt will be made in vicinity of BEHENCOURT FOR dinners. Battn. will resume march in afternoon.

[signature]
Captain.

Brigade Major.
11th Infantry Brigade.

20.5.16.

2nd Battn The Royal Irish Regt   Copy No ___
OPERATION   ORDER   No 22
                                                                The Field
Reference Maps LENS 11 & AMIENS 17   21-5-16

1. The Battalion will march to MORLANCOURT tomorrow
   Route - TALMAS - RUBEMPRÉ - BÉHENCOURT - FRANVILLERS - HEILLY - HALTE - MÉRICOURT - VILLE (sous CORBIE)

2. Starting Point road junction immediately East of R in BOIS MONSIEUR
   Order of march :- B - C - D - A.

3. Companies to be formed up at the starting point at 5 a.m.
   Officers kits to be dumped at the Q.M's store at 4 a.m.
   A halt will be made in the vicinity of BÉHENCOURT for breakfasts
   Tea will be issued at 4 a.m. before leaving billets

4. Reveille 3 a.m. Sick Parade 3.30 a.m.

                    Sd. T. A. Lowe, Capt & Adjt.
                    2/ The Royal Irish Regiment

Issued at 6 pm.
Copies to :-
  No.1 War Diary   No.6 Quartermaster
    2. O/C "A" Coy   7. Transport Off.
    3. " "B" "   8. Lewis R.O.
    4. " "C" "   9. R.S.M.
    5. " "D" "   10. Drums
                             11. Cook Sergt
                             12. Medical Officer

Lt Col Dugan DSO

Dear Colonel
    Your wire received at 3 am this morning just as we were moving off. If you will read the reverse you will see that we have left the 4th Divn and are going to MORLANCOURT to join the 7th, an amazing surprise to all concerned. I am sending 2 maps for your guidance & enclosing letters from Division which will explain everything. Major Gregory arrived on Thursday and is now commanding during your absence — it has been a strenuous time last week in every way. Will expect you to join us about 1 or 2 pm Sat

    Lowe

2nd Battalion The Royal Irish Regiment   Copy No 1
             Operation Order No 23

Reference Map France 62D NE   The Field 24/5/16

1. The Battalion will move to the camp in the BOIS D'ESTAILLES (K.12.a) this afternoon.

2. Companies will leave billets as under and will be guided straight to their respective huts —
   "B" Company _____ 6 pm
   "A"   "   _____ 6.5 "
   "D"   "   _____ 6.10 "
   "C"   "   _____ 6.15 "

3. All officers' kits will be dumped at Hdqrs and loaded up by 5.30 pm

4. Cookers and water carts will accompany the Battalion

                    (Sd) F.A. Lowry, Capt. & Adjt.
                    2/ The Royal Irish Regiment

Issued at 2 pm.
Copies to :—
   No 1 War Diary   No 7 Transport Offr
      2 O/C "A" Coy   8 Lewis G Offr
      3 " "B" "   9 Medical Offr
      4 " "C" "   10 R.S.M
      5 " "D" "   11 Coy Sgt
      6 Qrmr   12 Signals
                13 Drums

2nd Battn. The Royal Irish Regiment   Copy No. 1

Operation Order No 24

Reference Trench Map FRICOURT   The Field 26-5-16

1. The Battalion (less "A" Coy) will relieve the 2nd Bn. The Royal Warwickshire Regt in the trenches in C 2 sub sector on the 27th inst.

2. Companies will hold the line as follows:—
    Front line ————————————— B Coy
    Support (KINGSTON AV) ———— C "
    71 NORTH ————————————— D "

3. Companies will move into the line by platoons — 5 minutes interval between platoons — the leading platoon of companies, in above order, will move as follows —
    B Coy at 7.15 am
    D " " 8.15 "
    C " " 9.15 "

4. Officers trench kits will be stacked outside the H.Q. Guard by 8 am. Officers servants will accompany same. These will be brought to the trenches by the Regimental Transport. Officers spare kits will be stacked outside the canteen at the same hour and will be conveyed to the Q.M. Stores by the Regimental Transport. O.C. "A" Coy will arrange for these to be loaded up and off loaded at MORLANCOURT.

5. "A" Company and details attached, will parade at 9.30 am and proceed to billets in MORLANCOURT in relief of a company of the 2/Royal Warwicks. O.C. "A" Company will send advance party to MORLANCOURT to take over billets at 7.30 am and will also arrange for a rear party of 1 Officer and 15 other ranks to remain in camp after the departure of the Battalion and clean up the lines.

6. Lewis Rifles, Signallers, Scouts and Bombers will relieve the 2/Royal Warwicks under arrangements made by the officers concerned.

7.   Reveille 5 am
         Breakfast 6 am
         Sick Parade 6.30 am
    Commanding Officers Orders 7 am

                         continued

Operation Order No 24 continued

8. Battalion Headquarters will close in camp at 9 am and will re-open at J1 South at the same hour.

Sd T A Lowe Capt & Adjt
2/The Royal Irish Regt

Issued at 5 pm

Copy No. 1 War Diary
2 OC "A" Coy
3 OC "B" Coy
4 OC "C" Coy
5 OC "D" Coy
6 RM

No. 7 Transport Officer
8 Lewis Rifle Officer
9 Medical Officer
10 R.S.M.
11 Cook Sgt
12 Drums
13 O/C 2/R Warwick Regt (for infm)